𝕭𝖊𝖉𝖑𝖆𝖒 | ON THE JACOBEAN STAGE

ROBERT RENTOUL REED, JR.

1970

OCTAGON BOOKS
New York

PREFACE

I am particularly indebted to the Reverend Edward Geoffrey O'Donoghue's *The Story of Bethlehem Hospital* (1914) and to the physician Daniel Hack Tuke's *Chapters in the History of the Insane in The British Isles* (1882) for providing approximately thirty-five percent of the information included in the first chapter of this book. On the other hand, in presenting the history of both Bethlehem Hospital and the treatment of insanity during medieval times, I have, wherever possible, consulted other works and, in particular, the original sources of information. The Reverend Mr. O'Donoghue, however, as chaplain of Bethlehem Hospital, had access to a number of documents that are not available to me. Dr. Tuke, on his part, being a physician, made a somewhat more exhaustive study of the history of insanity in England than would be practical for me to do; my ultimate and basic purpose, by contrast to that of both my predecessors, is to interpret the persistent use of madness as a theatrical medium of the early seventeenth-century English playwright.

The reader will probably note that, in the analyses of many of the mad folk that are included in this book, both Elizabethan and modern terminologies are employed and that occasionally they appear side by side. In correlating the studies of mad folk with the influences of Elizabethan psychological theories, particularly as the latter were set forth by Timothy Bright and Robert Burton, I have, as far as possible, employed Elizabethan "humor" terminology. On the other hand, in the more complete analyses of characters, it has sometimes, for the sake of explicitness, been necessary to use such comparatively modern terms as *paranoia, dementia praecox, masochist,* and *sadism.* Indeed, even such common terms as *psychology, psychiatry,* and *pathology*—expressions which, together with their derivatives, are essential to an intelligible discussion of insanity—were unknown to the physician of the Jacobean period. If we consider the widespread interest of the Elizabethan and Jacobean in mental pathology, the paucity of psychiatric terminology becomes even more evident; we wonder how in some cases one physician could intelligibly communicate his ideas to another or how he could make out an accurate and comprehensible medical report on a patient. The truth is, as we learn from reading Bright in particular, that the Elizabethan could discuss the subject of insanity only in comparatively vague and general language; an insane person, for example, suffered from either *madness, phrenzie, melancholie,* or *dotage.* In order to make clear a madman's symptomatic behavior, the physician had few reasonably specific terms to which to resort and was compelled, as Burton often was, to rely upon extended illustrations of the patient's behavior. Consequently, although I cannot argue that our modern psychiatric terminology is the final achievement in explicitness, I have in many cases found it more specific than the Elizabethan.

In treating the mad folk of the Jacobean stage, I have excluded those of Shakespeare from analysis, although, in the course of this book, many references are made to them. The reader who is interested in interpretations of Shakespeare's madmen will find these remarkably penetrative studies of insanity quite amply treated by John Charles Bucknill, Henry Somerville, and other critics, whose works on this particular subject are included in the bibliography.

CONTENTS

BEDLAM ON THE JACOBEAN STAGE

1

When I think of the temper of the Jacobean stage, I sometimes picture a patient in the psychopathic ward running amuck with fever, his brains afire, as Robert Burton might have diagnosed him. Without undue exaggeration this mental image portrays the excitement, the temperature, and the precipitate career of Jacobean drama for the critic who, looking at it through the perspective of three hundred years, habitually compares it with the more conventional, and sometimes much less interesting, periods of dramatic literature that comprise the history of drama as a whole. The Jacobean stage was, and remains, distinguished by unusual abnormality, extravagance, and bombastic utterance; its average temper, figuratively speaking, was not a great deal short of madness, and if it occasionally lapsed into comparative conventionality, it did so generally only because a particular playwright, such as Heywood, could not or would not sustain the reckless pace of excitement that was demanded by the contemporary audience.

The purpose of this book will be to examine the use of insanity itself as a Jacobean theatrical device. I will undertake first to point out the external influences leading to the several types of portrayal of madness that are found in Jacobean drama; secondly, to interpret the mad folk both in their relation to Elizabethan psychopathic theory and as vehicles of theatricality; and, finally, to estimate the general importance of mad folk and distraught characters in so far as they contributed to the spirit and technique of Jacobean drama.

Several books and many articles about mad folk of the Jacobean theater have already been published, but all of these, with one notable exception, have been concerned almost entirely with studies of Shakespearean characters. The exception is E. A. Peers's book entitled *Elizabethan Drama And Its Mad Folk,* published in England in 1914. The work of Mr. Peers is confined primarily to an examination of the drama for information about the causes and treatment of insanity and, secondly, to a study of the mad folk "as pieces of art of intrinsic literary value." His book, creditable in its own aims, concerns itself neither with the origins of madness as a theatrical device nor with the relation of madness as a popular dramatic convention to the general extravagance of the Jacobean stage.

In reading and considering the works of John Charles Bucknill[1] and Henry Somerville,[2] both of whom were physicians, on Shakespearean mad folk and comparing their interpretations with one another as well as with those of Peers, the reader is likely to find himself in a state of confusion. In their diagnoses the two physicians and Mr. Peers disagree much more frequently than they agree. Somerville, for one example, believes Macbeth to be a "paranoiac" possessed of a "homicidal mania"; Peers and Bucknill, on the other hand, agree that Macbeth "escaped madness by rushing from the maddening horrors of meditation into a course of decisive resolute action." In regard to King Lear, Peers disagrees with the "medical men," who, he charges, almost invariably trace Lear's madness to circumstances predating the rise of the curtain. Peers's comment upon Lady Macbeth is that "her madness is fatal"; Bucknill, on the other hand, admits her breakdown, but insists that she was "scarcely insane." Somerville describes Constance's ultimate condition as "acute mania"; so had Bucknill; but Peers argues that she is never more than "half-crazy" and that therefore, by Elizabethan standards, she must be judged "sane." The mental condition of Hamlet is a public battleground where almost everybody disagrees. Of recent criticisms, Professor Oscar James Campbell's theory that Hamlet would today be diagnosed as a manic-depressive whose fluctuating moods invariably fail to fit the exigencies of the moment is perhaps one of the least ambitious and, consequently, one of the soundest interpretations.[3] In contrast, Dr. Ernest Jones's completely Freudian analysis[4] is a hundred-page masterpiece of induction, but it fails to convince this reader that Hamlet is suffering from a definitely marked "Oedipus complex." When we consider such matters as Hamlet's religious and moral convictions and his reasonable fear that the devil, in the form of his father's ghost, may be seeking to condemn his soul to hell, there is hardly cause to blame his hesitancy in carrying out the revenge motive upon the theory that he identified himself with his intended victim. There are, furthermore, other instances in early seventeenth-century drama of a revenger's failing to murder his enemy for the reason that the latter was, at the moment, too well prepared for heaven.

The preceding paragraph, which is indirectly a warning against making too precise interpretations of Jacobean mad folk, must also serve as an apology. Although one of the three purposes of this book will be an analytical interpretation of the mad folk that appeared on the Jacobean stage, no diagnosis, in the strictly modern sense at least, will be attempted. Instead, my efforts will be directed partly at interpreting the mad folk as theatrical devices and partly at correlating their symptoms with Elizabethan pathologic theory. A more professional diagnosis of the mad folk in drama is undoubtedly better left to the physicians, and even they do not always agree among themselves, a fact that is particularly true where the dramatic interpretation, as in the case of Hamlet, is most convincing. My conclusion is that insanity and mental disorders are so individualized that exact diagnosis is plausible only in the most stereotyped and obvious cases. Few critics or medical men are likely to agree, for instance, upon a definite diagnosis of Webster's Duke Ferdinand; but, in such a stereotyped example as Trouble-All of Jonson's *Bartholomew Fair,* it is probably safe to say that the large majority of critics would agree that he is a victim of monomania, for his tritely accentuated symptoms appear to preclude any other diagnosis.

I

Our first major problem will be to investigate the formative and professional influences that led to an abnormally extensive use of madness upon the Jacobean stage. Insanity, of course, was not a new theatrical device. The Greek tragedians and, later, Seneca had used it moderately. In medieval drama we can point to several depictions of Herod as examples of near madmen; and in the latter part of the Elizabethan period, beginning with Kyd's Hieronimo, at least six well-known madmen trod the boards of the early English theaters. But as yet there was no strong indication that the portrayal of madness had become an end in itself; that is, a theatrical attraction apart from its usefulness to story and plot construction. Hieronimo's madness, for example, is closely interwoven with the plot, as are both the brief insanity of Titus Andronicus and the delusional mania of Greene's Orlando. Consequently, the use of madness in drama before the time of *Hamlet* remained comparatively infrequent; there was, with the possible exception of Kyd's Isabella, no deliberate, and certainly no consistent, effort to introduce it upon the stage except in so far as it was closely integrated with the plot. Beginning with *Hamlet,* or about the year 1601, the deliberate and frequent use of insanity upon the English stage becomes increasingly apparent; more often than not, as in the "Bedlam" scenes of *The Honest Whore* and *Northward Ho,* it was used to produce a purely theatrical spectacle. Also, despite Shakespeare's masterful delineation, there appears reason to suspect that, particularly in his treatment of Ophelia and Lady Macbeth, he had become keenly aware of the theatrical appeal of madness. However subtle and perfect in portrayal, the insanity or mental derangement of neither woman, particularly Lady Macbeth, appears constructively essential to the main plot.

We may conclude that madness as a theatrical medium upon the English stage was neither frequently nor, as a rule, deliberately in use before the year 1601, a year that for dramatic purposes best marks the beginning of the Jacobean period. There is, moreover, another important difference between Elizabethan and Jacobean madness as depicted by the playwrights. Elizabethan mad folk were, like Hieronimo, little more than stereotyped renditions whose disordered minds were capable of imagining superhuman achievements. In this sense they were consistent with the Elizabethan superconfidence in the high destiny of man. Kyd, Greene, and the young Shakespeare were more inclined to emphasize the capabilities and achievements of mad folk than to examine and analyze insanity objectively. Hieronimo threatens to dig to the bowels of the Earth, Orlando likens himself to Hercules, Titus Andronicus threatens the gods and the heavens with his complaints; and, perhaps equally significant, each recovers to perform with complete sanity an act of culminating vengeance. Indeed, if we overlook his necessity to plot, the Elizabethan madman was little more than a mouthpiece for Elizabethan fustian. The Jacobean madman, on the other hand, was a much more objective study; he expressed the frustrations, not the potentialities, of mankind. Instead of aspiring to the superhuman, he almost always testified to the folly and impotency of human effort. Moreover, unlike the Elizabethan madman, he rarely, if ever, went mad without exhibiting a humor first, usually melancholy or choler; and, once mad, he rarely recovered his wits. However theatrical, he was, as a rule, a much more honest study than the Elizabethan madman. The Jacobean playwright, in brief, was not only more conscious of the theatrical appeal of madness than had been his Elizabethan predecessor, but he was also more sympathetic and understanding in its delineation.

On the one hand, then, the Jacobean playwright was to initiate a more genuine and pathologically sound interpretation of mad folk; on the other hand, theatricality seems definitely to have been the primary motive behind his consistent use of insanity. Consequently, as I have already indicated, he was also the first to make a widespread use of group madness, in which an honest interpretation of insanity was generally subordinated to the theatricality of the scene. Indeed, the nearest theatrical approach to mad folk en masse that predates the Jacobean stage appears to have been the medieval dramatic interpretations of Belial and his fellow devils, who sometimes were portrayed as howling and shrieking in fiendish delight around the maw of hell. Such interpretations, although they may have provided a hint for Jacobean playwrights, were too remote in spirit and conception to have been a formative influence on a stage that, in comedy at least, was basically documentary. To find and to analyze such an influence upon the interpretations of group madness, we must direct and then restrict our attention primarily to circumstances within the Jacobean period itself; meantime we must, of necessity, defer the discussion of the more profound dramatic presentations in which insane persons were represented.

II

The principal formative influence upon the theatrical presentations of group madness was undoubtedly Bethlehem Hospital and its inmates. If private asylums for the insane existed in London during Elizabethan and Jacobean times, there are no direct journalistic or literary allusions to them and therefore little likelihood that they were open to the public. Alibius's madhouse in *The Changeling* has often been considered a parody of a private institution; however, as will be pointed out later, it actually bears a striking similarity to Bethlehem both in its physical environment and in its management. Of the types of insane persons confined at Bethlehem Hospital in the early seventeenth century, we have little direct information; journalistic literature of the Jacobean period supplies us only the slightest information, and no contemporary medical reports remain. Therefore, although we shall first consider the historical background of Bethlehem Hospital, it will later be necessary to project our study and to examine the early eighteenth-century reports of visits to Bedlam by certain journalists, and, assuming that the types of inmates confined to the hospital had changed but little, judge the psychopathic ancestors by their descendants; secondly, and even more contrary to the usual procedure, we must then turn to the Jacobean dramatic presentations of Bedlamites and interpret the original through the copy. Then, perhaps, by putting two and two together, we shall have some idea of the inmate that the Elizabethan or Jacobean visitor may have witnessed within the reception hall or, more probably, within the cells themselves of the original Bethlehem Hospital.

In order better to understand the responsibilities and the functions of the Hospital, we shall turn back to feudal and even to Anglo-Saxon times and consider briefly the general theories and the treatments of madness as they were developed and practiced, respectively, throughout medieval England. Despite the extensive Elizabethan interest in psychology, insanity was not at that late date a new topic of interest in England. During medieval times, according to such authorities as Dr. Tuke and Dr. Walsh,[5] the care of the insane was an important responsibility of the monasteries; the topic of insanity, therefore, was undoubtedly (as the author of *Piers Plowman* indicates) an occasional concern to the individual Englishman, but particularly so if he were a churchman.

Long before the establishment of the royal and the public hospitals in England, the rank and file of the Christian medieval church had for centuries constituted what was perhaps the greatest single humanitarian organization that the Western world has known. Indeed, the nationwide care of the sick, the poor, and the underprivileged appears to have been in far better hands during England's medieval ages than at any other time until at least one hundred years after the Reformation. By 1150, according to Dr. Tuke, the monks were the only "medical practitioners" in England. Perhaps even before this date, but certainly subsequently, the understanding and the care of the mentally ill were considered essential and necessary parts of the holy man's training.

Bartholomew de Glanville, an English friar minor of the thirteenth century and the author of the *De Proprietatibus Rerum,* which has been referred to as a "compendium of information for monks," was mindful of the foregoing monastic responsibility for the mentally afflicted and wrote a highly illuminating paragraph upon the insane. The causes of insanity, as enumerated by Bartholomew, were: extreme anxiety "as of business and great thoughts," excessive sorrows, too extensive studies, fear, the bite of a mad dog or of some other "venomous beast," strong wine, and "melancholy meats." He divided symptoms into two broad categories: some victims "cry, leap, and injure"; others are "dark" and secretive. By comparison to heartlessly unsympathetic practices three hundred years later, Bartholomew's recommendations for treatment were touchingly humane: binding only if the patient were dangerous; refreshing entertainment and comfort; removal from the original environment of the patient's insanity; and lastly, music and occupation. Indeed, this lonely friar minor was at least five hundred years ahead of his time in the humanity and, particularly, in the sensibleness of the treatment which he advocated. The regimen of the monks, compared to the neglect and severity following the Reformation in the 1530's, was humane and sympathetic; but, despite the modern and sensible tone of Bartholomew's advice, the actual medical treatment of the insane, however charitable, was to remain the "curious compound of pharmacy, superstition, and castigation"[6] that it had been, indeed, ever since early Anglo-Saxon times.

III

The Saxons had regarded most forms of insanity, particularly phrenitis—or brain fever—and the more aggravated types of melancholia, such as dementia and delusional insanity, as "devil sickness"; consequently, whipping, as a means of castigation, had from the earliest times been an accepted, and unfortunately popular, method of seeking to drive the devil from a possessed person. For this purpose, as Dr. Tuke tells us, "a skin of mereswine [porpoise]" was worked into a whip.[7] There were, however, other and far more intricate methods of eradicating the devil from the possessed; most of these forms of treatment combined an involved mixture of pharmacy with a high degree of superstition. Among Saxon and later medieval prescriptions, we find compounds of such herbs as lupin, bishopwort, henbane, and cropleek pounded together, then mixed with ale (perhaps to make the mixture palatable); this concoction then stood overnight, holy water was added, and, finally, while a priest on certain occasions recited invocations over him, the patient drank it. The "classic peony," to quote Tuke, and the mandrake were also traditionally used for the treatment of the insane. In the application of many herbal mixtures, the phase of the moon was regarded as a dominant consideration if the cure were to be effected. Laertes, in *Hamlet,* is perhaps mindful of this tradition when he observes:

I bought an unction of a mountebank,
So mortal that . . .
Where it draws blood no cataplasm so rare,
Collected from all simples that have virtue
Under the moon, can save the thing from death.

In later medieval times, "bowssening"—that is, immersing the patient in a well—became one of the most popular treatments of the insane. The patient, we are told, was first doused, then bound and left overnight upon the cold floor of a chapel or, if no chapel was convenient, upon an outdoor altar. This procedure, as a rule, was repeated several times until either the devil was forcibly washed out or hope of effecting the cure was abandoned. Scotland and northern England, notably Northumberland, appear to have specialized in "bowssenings." Supporting this legendary, but fairly sound, conclusion, Tuke quotes Scott's "Marmion":

Then to Saint Fillan's blessed well,
Whose spring can frenzied dreams dispel
And the crazed brain restore.

Saint Fillan's well in Scotland, as is further pointed out by Tuke, is referred to, not once, but several times, in the literature of the eighteenth century as a traditional, although probably not contemporary, shrine for the treatment and alleged cure of the insane.[8]

In addition to castigation, herbal concoctions, and "bowssening," there were several other popular methods of treating the "devil sickness" that appear to have been recurrently practiced in medieval times. Tuke informs us, for example, that in England and Scotland lunatics were sometimes bound to a cross, such as "Saint Mangose Crosse" in Scotland, and left there overnight and "in the morning often found sane and whole."[9] Undoubtedly, as supported by the addition of holy water to certain compounds and the placing of the patient on a chapel floor following "bowssening," the theory that divine influence was instrumental in driving out the devil had survived its Oriental origin and become a prevalent belief in Christian Europe. In one superstitious practice, however, there seems to have been no trace either of physical or of theological influences; indeed, the burying of live cocks under the ground as a cure for the madness of a human being, a treatment that was several times alluded to by medieval practitioners, appears to have been the product of crass superstition.

The dark-room treatment appears to have been medieval in its origin, but the first definite reference to it that I have found is in Dr. Borde's *A Compendious Rygment or Dyetry of Helth,* which was published in 1542. For the cure of lunacy Dr. Borde particularly recommended a "chamber where there is lytell light" and "a keeper the whiche the madde men do feare." Together with whipping and the various compounds of herbs, both of which had their origins in classical times, if not earlier, the treatment by confinement in a dark room was to survive its probable medieval origin to become one of the chief methods for the treatment of the insane in both Elizabethan and seventeenth-century England.

Little information about medieval theories of the causes and the symptoms of insanity is extant. Where causes more convincing than the idea of possession by a devil are concerned, the comparatively long list of external causes that Bartholomew enumerated is quite obviously commonplace, even though it comprises a reasonably large part, ironically enough, of our present-day knowledge. In addition, however, to this friar minor's commonsense conclusions, a few comparatively professional theories relative to causes appear to have been active, particularly after 1100; undoubtedly, for the most part, they were based more on superstition than on sound medical knowledge. At least one man, however, Giraldus of Wales, writing in the twelfth century, and very likely concurring with other medieval physicians, recognized the influence of disordered humors (for example, black or yellow bile) upon mental disease. Indeed, according to Dr. Tuke, Giraldus is the first Briton to mention the humors. Unfortunately, on the other hand, like his fellow physicians, Giraldus could not escape the traditional superstition that the full moon was one of the primary causes of madness; consequently, the humors of Giraldus, sensible in themselves, were sup-

posedly activated and disordered by lunar phases rather than by
the functional disorders of the body. Indeed, despite the apparent
good sense shown in Bartholomew's list of external causes, the late
medieval mind found it difficult to disassociate the pathology of
mental disease from the universal superstition that madness was
externally determined by the moon, especially by its full phase.

If, then, in late medieval times the humors, activated by the
moon, were considered a primary cause of insanity, why did the
people, for the most part, still persist in believing that the majority
of mad folk were devil-possessed? The fact is that the two theories,
the humor theory and the idea of devil-possession, appear to have
been awkwardly correlated and, in a tenuous relationship, they
survived not only well into Elizabethan times, but, when reinforced
by the persistent belief in witchcraft, well through the seventeenth
century. Bright, despite his scientific attitude toward madness, explicitly states, in chapter 33 of *A Treatise of Melancholie,* that
Satan, or the devil, is forever hankering after melancholic persons.
In adopting this idea he is betraying his deference to tradition
because it is certainly inconsistent with his other theories, particularly with the hypothesis that the conscience of God, in contrast to the influence of the devil, strikes directly at the human soul
without respect to the condition or corruption of the humors. We
may, therefore, conclude that the development of pathological
theory, particularly in Elizabethan times, merely jeopardized but
did not altogether destroy the ancient Saxon doctrine of "devil sickness." This particular incongruity that resulted from medieval tradition and awkwardly correlated mental pathology with devil-possession not only left an imprint upon the psychological conclusions
of Bright and Burton, but also recurrently cropped up in the contemporary drama and is particularly evident in such Jacobean
plays as *The Devil Is An Ass, The Yorkshire Tragedy,* and, ultimately, *The Witch of Edmonton,* in which not only the melancholic

Mother Sawyer is possessed, but two other pathologically unstable persons are driven to frenzy or, in Frank's case, to irresponsible action by immediate contact with the devil.

IV

Bethlehem Hospital was not established initially as an asylum for the insane. The institution, originally known as St. Mary of Bethlehem, had been founded in 1247 as a priory on property formerly owned by Simon FitzMary, who had twice been sheriff of London. This property, deeded by FitzMary to the see of Bethlehem, the mother church of which was in Palestine, was located just outside Bishops Gate in the northerly parish of St. Botolph.

The first mention of the little priory of St. Mary of Bethlehem as a hospital, but not as an asylum, is found in a royal grant signed by Edward III in 1329; this grant extended the right to collect alms. Both in caring for the sick and in supporting its charitable work by the collection of alms, St. Mary's priory was merely following the tradition of hundreds of priories and monasteries throughout medieval Europe. Edward's reference to it as a hospital, however, indicates that the care of the sick had become its primary function and responsibility. Serving the public welfare is not, however, a usually profitable business when measured in shillings and pounds; consequently, in 1346, little Bethlehem, still officially registered as a priory despite its apparently extensive care of the sick, was forced to petition for help and, at the same time, to complain of disaster, neglect, and "continual disrepute." As a result, the city council of London extended its protection and assumed for the first time the full responsibility of maintaining the little priory—not for a day or a year, but "for ever." Officially, therefore, in 1346 Bethlehem became the ward, but not the property, of the city of London. This wardship, however, was to last less than thirty years. Since its founding, the priory had legally remained the property, however neglected, of the bishop of Bethlehem, who resided in Clamency, France; in 1375, therefore, during the French wars, Edward III seized it as an alien priory. Subsequently, for nearly two hundred years, little Bethlehem, despite the recurrent protest of the citizens of London, who apparently did not forget their short-lived guardianship, was to remain under the control and, as a rule, niggardly patronage of the kings of England.

Not long after its seizure by the English crown, Bethlehem, already experienced in the care of the sick, began, insignificantly at first, its long career as an asylum for the insane. John Stow, the Elizabethan chronicler, mentions both "an house" at Charing Cross and a hospital in the parish of Barking[10] as medieval asylums predating the transformation of Bethlehem to an institution for the insane. Furthermore, according to a report made by the commissioners of Bethlehem in 1632, the hospital had formerly owned a house, called the Stone House, at Charing Cross, and this house "was sometimes employed for the harbouring of mad and distracted persons before such time as they were removed to the present house of Bethlehem."[11] Since Stow also informs us that "said house by Charing Crosse" belonged to Bethlehem, it is almost certain that the house mentioned by him was the Stone House. There can be no doubt, consequently, that, even before the transfer of patients, which took place sometime between 1377 and 1403, Bethlehem was at least indirectly concerned with the care of the insane. Speaking of the transfer of the insane from the "house by Charing Crosse" to Bethlehem, Stow wrote: "It was said that some time a king of England not liking such a kind of people to remain so near his palace, caused them to be removed further off to Bethlehem."[12] As Tuke reminds us, there never was a royal palace near Charing Cross; on the other hand, we learn from Stow that a falcon house belonging to the king was erected at Charing Cross in 1375. It is, therefore, probable that either Richard II or Henry IV, upon visiting the falconry, complained of the disturbance made by the mad folk and, consequently, requested their removal "further off to Bethlehem."

The transfer of patients to the priory of Bethlehem was unquestionably carried out before 1403, in which year Henry IV brought thirty-five indictments against Peter Taverner, porter of what may henceforth be accurately termed Bethlehem Hospital; in the report of the royal commission appointed to investigate the defendant, six insane inmates are mentioned.[13] Peter was apparently the first of several officers of the hospital who were to exploit the mental limitations of the patients; he was fined £100 and dismissed.

The affairs at large of Bethlehem Hospital do not appear to have progressed very favorably under the patronage of the crown. In 1437, the new master felt obliged to report that the grounds were in disrepair and that divine services were almost at an end. Meanwhile, the institution appears to have become more of a political pawn than anything else; several of the royal chaplains and even a devoted physician, apparently having outlived their usefulness at court, were at different times "rewarded" with the mastership of "Our Lady of Bedlam."

During the reign of Henry VIII, the royal hospitals appear to have been exploited and taxed more excessively than ever. Partially, perhaps, but not entirely, as a result of this mistreatment, the city renewed its efforts to regain those institutions which it had formerly lost to the crown. After several petitions, and for a tidy sum of money, London succeeded in buying back from the necessitous king, only a few months before his death in 1547, several hospitals and institutions that his predecessors had by fraud or by political redress acquired for nothing; among these institutions was "Bethlem." There was, however, another and undoubtedly more significant reason for the insistence of the city council in petitioning for the return and control of Bethlehem as well as of one or two other hospitals. In 1538, the council had made its first petition for the control and government of Bethlehem Hospital; in this petition it was significantly alleged that the suppression of the churches had reduced "the sick, lame, and impotent poor . . . to great distress."[14]

Shortly after its transfer back to the people of London in 1547, and mainly as a result of the closing down of the monasteries, which from time out of mind had been a refuge for the mentally diseased, Bethlehem Hospital seems to have assumed a progressively greater responsibility in the housing and the treatment of the insane; on the other hand, its financial resources do not appear to have improved sufficiently to maintain this burden of increased public service. In 1557 Bethlehem was placed under the management of Bridewell Hospital, probably, as it seems, to reduce the costs of administration. Subsequently, throughout Elizabethan and Jacobean times, in fact, until its eventual transfer to Moorfields in 1676, recurrent investigations revealed only two general conditions—neglect and mismanagement—both of which apparently resulted from insufficient income. In 1598, an inspection party representing the board of governors made a report entitled "A View of Bethlehem" and dated December 4th, which presents perhaps our most informative picture of the hospital in Elizabethan times. Not only does the report inform us that twenty insane persons were in residence, but the inspection party's conclusion was that the insane ward "was so loathesomely and filthily kept that it was not fit for any man to come into said house." If "said house" was actually as revolting as this report suggests, we are led to wonder why the hospital and its mad folk during Elizabethan times were considered one of the chief amusements within the immediate environments of the city of London. Undoubtedly, however, the report of the inspection party had a beneficial effect; indeed, its very phraseology, upon careful examination, seems to suggest some immediate concern for the public's regular patronage of the hospital.

"In the Reign of Queen Elizabeth," to quote John Stow—but more exactly, according to O'Donoghue, in the year 1575—the church and chapel that had for centuries stood in or at the rear of the rectangle enclosed by the two parallel wings of the hospital were torn down. With their removal passed the last substantial trace of the priory. Stow tells us that houses were erected in their place; "houses," however, in the customarily lax Elizabethan phraseology, could well have included two or three apartments, which appear to have been added about this time along the open end on the west side of the hospital. If we consider the sketch that W. Hollar made of Bethlehem in 1667, then remove from it the additions built in 1644 and 1662, respectively, we can determine a physical layout of the hospital that is also consistent with Agas's sketch in his map of London (1560). In late Elizabethan times, the hospital formed a rectangle, the front of which faced eastward on Bishops Gate Street, just without the gate itself; in this part of the hospital, over-looking the street, were, respectively, both the steward's and the porter's houses and between them an open yard. On the north and south, respectively, running east to west away from the front, were two long wings, making with the front portion a U-shape; in each of these two wings, on the ground floors, there appear to have been ten cells, or twenty all told; the north wing also included the kitch-en and the south, apparently in its forward part nearest Bishops Gate Street, seems to have contained the reception room. Adjacent to the northwest corner of the north wing, and farthest from the street, was a barn, where the straw for the patients' bedding was kept. The new apartments, apparently erected shortly after 1575, only partially enclosed the west end. So much for the physical lay-out; now let us consider briefly the environs of the hospital. Diagon-

ally and a bit southward across Bishops Gate Street, according to
Agas's map and as indicated both by Stow's *Survey of London* and
by Dekker's and Webster's *Northward Ho,* was the Dolphin, "a
large Inn for the Receipt of Travellers"; on the south side, between
the hospital and the city wall, stood St. Botolph's church; to the west
was Depe-Ditch, and to the north, private property. According to
O'Donoghue, a dirt road ran east and west between the hospital
and St. Botolph's church; consequently, a second entrance, on the
south side, may have led the visitor directly to the parlor of the
hospital.

Bethlehem Hospital, as indicated by the replacement of the church
by houses and small apartments, had begun by 1575 a necessary
period of expansion. Not only was the population of London increasing, but, as I have said, the closing down of the monasteries
in the late 1530's had indirectly placed a much heavier burden upon
the hospital. Late in the eighteenth century King George III of England was to appoint a board called the Commissioners for Inquiring
Concerning Charities. According to both Tuke and Charles Knight
in his *Cyclopedia of London,*[15] these commissioners discovered an
unusually informative extract, made in the "muniment book" in
1632; this extract, moreover, not only provides our earliest first-hand
description of the actual interior structure of the hospital, but, in
correlation with other information, helps to confirm our supposition that Bethlehem was expanding. According to the extract, the
old house in the year 1632 contained "below stairs a parlour, a kitch-
en, two larders, a long entry through the house, and twenty-one
rooms wherein the poor distracted people lie, and above stairs eight
rooms more for the servants and poor to lie in."[16] In 1598, as we
have learned from the inspection party's report cited above, Bethlehem housed twenty inmates, fourteen of whom were private patients, while the remaining six, as we are told, were charity cases.
Furthermore, we are authoritatively informed by the commissioners'

report dated October 10, 1632 and addressed by the president and treasurer of Bethlehem to the Privy Council[17] that the hospital now contained twenty-seven distracted persons; in fact, a year earlier the board of governors had reported thirty inmates.[18] As far as I can determine, the eight rooms "above stairs" were by this time, at least in part, being used as an insane ward. As we know that the total number of patients had increased from twenty in 1598 to approximately thirty and that only one patient, as a rule, was permitted to a cell or a room, it seems likely, in consideration of the fact that there were only twenty-one rooms on the ground floor, that several of either the milder insane cases or, more likely, the charity patients were, by 1632, housed "above stairs." Bethlehem, now a hospital for the insane, had no obligation to the "poor" proper; nor, because of excessive demands to take care of the mentally diseased, could it very well assume such an additional, even though charitable, obligation.

Before its transfer in 1676 to Moorfields, old and now comparatively tumbled-down Bethlehem once again expanded. By a court order of 1643, accommodations for twenty more patients were added on the west side, overlooking Depe-Ditch. These accommodations, which at best only indirectly concern the Jacobean period, were completed in 1644.

We have seen that the hospital was obliged to house an increasing number of patients during Elizabethan and Jacobean times; I have also said that the necessity to expand its facilities resulted in a heavy, and sometimes insupportable, financial burden. According to Stow, for example, in 1551, only four years after the city of London had assumed the legal ownership of the hospital, Edward VI granted protection to John Whitehead, proctor of Bethlehem, to beg alms within the counties of Lincoln and Cambridge, the city of London, and the Isle of Ely; "Which," as Stow promptly reminds us, "was a Sign the revenues of it were now become but small, and not able to maintain the Charge." Very probably the revenues were no less than they had been under the kings of England; on the other hand, however, the need for expanding the hospital's facilities, an urgency enforced by the Reformation and the subsequent closing down of the monasteries, seems to have considerably augmented "the Charge" and, consequently, necessitated a progressively greater source of revenue.

In 1561 the court of Aldermen found it necessary to establish a commission for "the survey, ordering, and letting to farm the house of Bethlehem and the lands and possessions of the same."[19] We know from the commissioners' report of 1632 that as early as 1555 Bethlehem had a "settled income" of a little more than £34 a year and that this income was presumably from the rental of property.[20] The establishment, however, of the commission of 1561 strongly suggests that the present income from property was not sufficient to meet expenses, that some property may have still remained unaccounted for, and that circumstances were considered so bad as to warrant the letting of "the house of Bethlehem" itself. I find no evidence that the hospital proper was ever rented, but many years later King James was to exercise direct control over the hospital.[21] In 1618, for example, the king personally engineered the removal of Thomas Jenner from the mastership of Bethlehem: three months later, he appointed one of his private court physicians, Dr. Hilkiah Crooke, as Jenner's successor.

Despite the fact that King James appears to have exercised, when he wished, direct control over the management of the hospital, its revenues in proportion to its growing responsibility had certainly not improved. In 1622, the president and the governors of Bethlehem issued a statement that the revenues of the hospital were "insufficient to meet expenses." Ten years later, it was once more confirmed that the hospital, despite the fact that its "settled income" was now more than £277 a year, was unable to carry out its obligations.

Worst of all, however, years of hardship and niggardly financing had led, indirectly at least, to corruption and neglect within the hospital. Dr. Crooke, for one, unable to support himself or to maintain his steward out of the comparatively slender salary afforded by the governors, had neglected his duties, appearing "but once a quarter to receive his money," and had left the steward to make his own living at the expense of the unhappy inmates. While the steward fattened himself and his pockets by misappropriating "casual gifts" and allowances, the patients, according to the commissioners' report of 1632, went without food for several days on end.[22] As the report implies, this apparently was not an entirely new situation; a year earlier, in 1631, two governors upon an inspection tour of Bethlehem had observed that the patients were "like to starve."

In dismissing Thomas Jenner and replacing him with Dr. Crooke, King James had perhaps acted according to the humanitarian dictates of his conscience. Jenner was not a physician; there had apparently been repeated complaints of neglect and mistreatment of the patients; following an investigation, the king ordered his commissioners to "dislodge any person who lacks the necessary skill, and to raise Bethlehem to the level of St. Bartholomew's and St. Thomas's [both of which were hospitals]."[23] Bethlehem, however, had only rarely before been under the immediate charge of a physician; neglect, consequently, cannot be blamed entirely upon the fact that Jenner was "unskilful in the practice of medicine."[24] According to a document collected in *Remembrancia,* the hospital, unable consistently to meet its financial obligations, was in no position either to offer lucrative employment for its officers or to provide the essentials of food and medicines necessary to the proper care of the patients.[25] In 1620, moreover, two years after the removal of the nonphysician Jenner, "The Petition of the Poor Distracted People in the House of Bedlem" was registered in Stationers' Hall. This pamphlet is lost; but, according to O'Donoghue, contemporaneous court records support its tenor: a father charged that his daughter's foot was rotting away because of neglect by the officers and servants of the hospital; sundry charges were brought against the servants of the institution for unnecessary severity toward the patients. The unhappy situation implied by these charges is emphasized by a court order[26] more than twenty years later, wherein the court was compelled to forbid the giving of blows or ill language "to any of the mad folk" by an officer or servant of the hospital "on pain of losing his place." Apparently, therefore, the removal of Thomas Jenner in favor of the physician Dr. Crooke, whose own administration ended in the near starvation of the inmates, did not eradicate the fundamental causes of mismanagement, which appear largely to have been financial difficulties. The journalist Donald Lupton, writing at the end of the Jacobean period, has left us a vivid, if possibly exaggerated, picture of the resultant consternation among the inmates. "It seems strange," wrote Lupton, "that any one should recover here, the cryings, screechings, roarings, brawlings, shaking of chaines, swearings, frettings, chaffings, are so many, so hideous, so great" that, as Lupton concludes, a man was more likely to lose his wits than to regain them.[27]

V

Shortly we shall consider the mad folk, the Bedlamites, themselves. But first, assuming that we were a Jacobean, what might our chances be of actually visiting the hospital? The earliest reference that I have found in literature to an actual visit to Bethlehem is one by Thomas More in his treatise *The Four Last Things* (*c.* 1522)—a reference in which he also gives us a picture of one type of mad folk that we might expect to find in Bedlam. "Think not," wrote More, "that everything is pleasant that men for madness laugh at. For thou shalt in Bedleem see one laugh at the knocking of his head against a post, and yet there is little pleasure therein."[28] Of Elizabethan and

Jacobean visits to Bethlehem Hospital, journalistic literature has left us only the slimmest account; indeed, the great majority of Jacobean references to Bethlehem as a place of amusement are found in the drama. Besides Lupton's report of visiting Bethlehem, there remains, however, at least one other purely documentary record of a Jacobean visit. According to an excerpt that O'Donoghue has published in the appendix of his book, "Lord Percy with Lady Penelope and her two sisters 'saw the lions [in the Tower], the show of Bethlehem, the place where the prince was created, and the fireworks at the Artillery Gardens.' "[29] In the latter part of the seventeenth century, both Evelyn and Pepys in their diaries made reference to visits to Bethlehem Hospital; of these, Evelyn's report, dated April 21, 1657, is the more illuminating. "I stepped into Bedlam, where I saw several poor miserable creatures in chains; one of them was mad with making verses."

In the drama of the Jacobean period, as I have said, is found the most extensive evidence of the contemporary popularity of Bethlehem Hospital as a place of amusement. In at least three relatively documentary plays—*The Honest Whore,* Part I, in which the Duke sets out "as if to see the lunatics," *Northward Ho,* and *The Pilgrim*—the principal actors, through the playwright's contrivance, eventually find their way to Bethlehem in order to amuse themselves in Jacobean fashion with the antics of the inmates. In two other plays, *The Duchess of Malfi* and *The Changeling,* the inmates of an insane asylum go through their harebrained routine, climaxed by the customary morris dance; furthermore, Alibius's madhouse, which is the asylum in *The Changeling,* may well be a caricature of Bethlehem itself. In Ford's *Lover's Melancholy,* principal actors masquerade as Bedlamites. Elsewhere in Jacobean drama there are recurrent allusions to visits to Bethlehem Hospital. In *Bartholomew Fair* we learn at the outset that Dame Purecraft has been to Bedlam twice to inquire whether or not any lunatics are available for marriage; a little later in the same play, Wasp inquires of Dame Overdo, "How sharpe you are! with being at Bet'lam yesterday?"[30] In *The Silent Woman,* Bedlam is suggested by the ladies of The College as being, together with the Exchange and the China houses, a somewhat risqué and therefore desirable place for feminine amusement; a little earlier in this play, Truewit informs the recluse Morose that the "mad-folks" are one of the "daily" sights of the city.[31] In support of the tenor of this suggestion, the hero in Fletcher's *The Pilgrim* is all but plucked off a street corner by a sympathetic citizen and in‐ vited to visit the madhouse, presumably Bethlehem, which is refer‐ red to "as one of the sights of the city." In Middleton's *A Mad World, My Masters,* Sir Bounteous suspects that his grandson was married in the hospital: "When was the wedding kept? In Bed‐ lam?"[32] Inasmuch as two of the principal actors in *The Honest Whore,* Part I, are actually married at "Bethlehem Monastery," which in the play immediately adjoins the hospital, we are led to wonder whether or not, after the church was torn down in 1575, the hospital did not continue in some form or another its former religious rites and practices. Be that as it may, the repeated testimony of Jacobean drama, even if it remained unsupported by other evi‐ dence, such as Lord Percy's visit and, later, that of Lupton, appears to be sufficient in itself to prove that Bethlehem Hospital was not only regularly open to the public, but also had actually become one of the more talked-about and popular amusements of the city.

In addition to the many direct allusions to visits to Bethlehem, and besides, what is more important, the hospital's use as a setting in at least three plays, there are recurrent references in the drama of the period that indicate a familiar knowledge of the function and the responsibilities of the hospital. Dekker, in *Westward Ho,* for example, uses the expression "as dark as a roome in Bedlam." Shakespeare's Rosalind compares love to "madness," which "deserves as well a dark house and a whip as madmen do."[33] Malvolio, in

Twelfth Night, is locked in a dark room because he is allegedly possessed by the "hyperbolical fiend." In Dekker and Middleton's *Roaring Girl,* Sir Alexander observes: "Bedlam cures not more madmen in a year, Than one of the Counters does."[34] These references, of course, are perhaps more directly concerned with the methods or results of treatment; but, supported by the references of the preceding paragraph, they help to confirm the supposition that the playwrights were personally, as members of the public, familiar not only with Bethlehem's popularity as a place of amusement, but also with its interior environment.

In estimating the extent of Bethlehem's popularity as an amusement center, we must consider the fact that during the eighteenth century, if not at a much earlier date, the income from public admissions was one of the major sources of the hospital's revenues. Upon good authority, including that of Tuke and O'Donoghue, we know that Bethlehem eventually enjoyed an annual income of at least £400 a year from visitors alone before the doors were closed to the public once and for all in 1770. Our best authority, however, is Thomas Bowen's pamphlet entitled "An Historical Account of Bethlehem Hospital," which was published in 1783, only thirteen years after the closing down of "the penny gates." Bowen, who had been an on-the-scene observer, wrote: "The hospital used formerly to derive a revenue of at least £400 a year from the indiscriminate admission of visitants." This, of course, would mean that 96,000 persons at a penny apiece visited the hospital annually. As the result of a court order in 1657, the doors of Bethlehem had been closed to the public on Sundays;[35] therefore, during the eighteenth century and on the basis of a probable six-day week, Bethlehem apparently enjoyed an average of three hundred visitors a day. Tuke, however, felt that so large a patronage was an excessively high figure; consequently, citing a passage from Ned Ward's *London Spy* (1703), he concluded, with uncertain confidence, however, that the admission was twopence and that, consequently, there were only 48,000 visitors a year, which, to Tuke, was a much more satisfactory figure. But Tom Brown, a contemporary of Ward, plainly states in *London Amusements* that the admission was a penny.[36] Moreover, the visit that Ward reported was made in the company of a friend; in describing their departure from the hospital, Ward wrote: "After redeeming our liberties from this prison at the expense of twopence, we were led by our appetites into a cook's shop."[37] Ward, I might add, had paid nothing, according to his account, upon entering the hospital. There appears to be only one sensible conclusion to his statement quoted above: two people were able to depart from the hospital at the price of twopence, or for a penny apiece.

If, then, in the eighteenth century, 96,000 persons visited Bethlehem annually, we may conclude that, in view of the evident popularity of the hospital in Jacobean times, the patronage at this earlier date was a fairly large one, but certainly far below that of a century later, by which time the population of London had more than trebled. Furthermore, the magnificence of the new hospital at Moorfields, which Brown admiringly compared to the Louvre, must have attracted certain persons of taste that probably would have shunned the old house of Bethlehem with its antiquated and sometimes "loathesome" interior. With these points in mind, we may assume that the hospital in Jacobean times attracted, at very best, only 30 percent as many visitors as did the eighteenth-century hospital. But, regardless of the smaller patronage, averaging probably less than seventy-five visitors a day, it was this old house of Bedlam, not the new one, that was to exert an influence on English dramatic literature second to that of no other similar institution.

VI

What then, in particular, were the symptoms and peculiar eccentricities that lured the Jacobean visitor to see the mad folk? As already stated, we learn little or nothing of the type of inmate from contemporaneous journalistic reports; we must turn, therefore, to the comic drama of the Jacobean period and to the journalistic reports of Brown, Ward, and Steele of the early eighteenth century and then, after making due allowance for a general tone of exaggeration, draw our own conclusions regarding the symptoms that confronted and sometimes fascinated the Jacobean visitant to the hospital.

First of all, let us turn to the accounts of the eighteenth-century journalists; by eliminating much of the comical elaboration, we can get perhaps an approximate picture of the inmate of the new Bethlehem, who probably differed very little from his psychopathic ancestor of the old hospital ninety to one hundred years earlier. Brown, who has left us the least actual detail, reported among others the following inmates: a lawyer who was a victim of monomania; a Jacobite who suffered from maniacal frenzy, but whom a favorable change of government probably would have cured; a scholar who went mad in the pursuit of knowledge; and a melancholic Whig "bemoaning his want of office."[38] Ned Ward, in his account of the inmates, has left us considerably more detailed information, much of it exaggerated, but more instructive than Brown's. The first case that Ward, upon visiting Bethlehem, observed was one of delusional insanity, which seems to have been an especially common type at Bethlehem; this particular inmate considered himself "Prince of the Air" and apparently was not to be dissuaded from his conviction. Ward next was attracted to the cell of a demented prankster; this patient made idiotic comments upon the bread and cheese that he was munching and then counterfeited a sneeze, with unfortunate results for the bystanders, but to his own great mirth. The third patient, as reported by Ward, was a melancholic Cambridge scholar, who had once been highly proficient in music. Ward's fourth, and possibly most interesting, madman was a victim of phrenitis, who raved one moment and the next trampled down Conscience as "fierce as a lion" under his feet. A fifth inmate, who seems to have been a political prisoner as much as a sufferer from a mild case of phrenitis, spoke vehemently against the monarchy, then intelligently explained that only within Bedlam and by the mad folk could the truth be spoken with immunity.[39] In summary, Ward has presented to us a patient with delusional insanity, a prankster who was probably suffering from dementia, a melancholic scholar, and two patients with phrenitis. Indeed, there appears some question whether or not the fifth inmate, who, as Ward reported, raved against the monarchy, was actually insane. He suggests a practice that had apparently been employed in Elizabethan and Jacobean times, a recurrent policy of assigning political malcontents to Bethlehem Hospital. In 1595, for example, a silkweaver "came to the Lord Mayor's house, using some hard speeches . . . in dispraise of his government," and was promptly pronounced to be "mad" by the mayor, who then ordered that he be "committed . . . to Bedlam."[40] Some years later, for a very similar reason, King James confined a recalcitrant officer named Weekes to the hospital.[41]

We should not, of course, give too much credence to the reports of Brown and Ward, neither of whom, having his reading public in mind, could avoid some satirical and spirited elaboration. But the fundamental symptoms of the mad folk seem to be authentically reported; else, we might ask, what basis would the journalist have to elaborate upon the inmates of the hospital? We can, however, depend considerably less upon the observations of Isaac Bickerstaff, the hero of *The Tatler* and, although a pseudonym for Richard Steele, primarily a fictitious character. According to Bickerstaff, the new Bethlehem at Moorfields had "some years ago" the honor of housing "five dutchesses, three earls, two heathen gods, an emperor, and a prophet." Furthermore, a fat tailor's wife, if we wish to believe Bickerstaff, was no other in her confirmed opinion than the "Lady Mayoress" of London.[42] The supposition to be derived from these observations is that a good many patients with delusional insanity, whether paranoia or a symptom of dementia praecox, were regularly confined in Bethlehem Hospital; but whether or not "five dutchesses" and "two heathen gods" were actually interned at one and the same time is a matter that is undoubtedly best left to the conscience of Isaac Bickerstaff.

Even to a greater degree than the journalist, the playwright has persistently exercised the creative artist's prerogative of exaggeration. But Jacobean comedy, as a rule, is documentary as well as theatrical; consequently, we may presume that the playwrights' depictions of Bedlamites were constructed about a reasonably sound foundation of actual observation. In the next chapter, the comic presentations of group madness will be discussed at much greater length. For the moment, it is sufficient to summarize the symptoms and eccentricities of the Bedlamites as presented upon the Jacobean stage and, correlating these summaries with those of Brown, Ward, and the fictitious Isaac Bickerstaff, to arrive at and confirm a general estimate of the symptomatic behavior of the actual inmates of the hospital.

Dekker, in *The Honest Whore,* Part I, produced in 1604, was the first playwright to bring Bedlam directly to the stage. Despite a theatrical necessity to exaggerate the comic aspects of the Bedlamite, Dekker, as was his habit, appears to have relied upon a solid core of first-hand observation. In this play, Dekker introduces three mad folk. The first, a merchant, has suffered an unexpected reversal; in consequence, he has become a monomaniac whose mind is primarily preoccupied with a closely related group of ideas that surround the loss of his "five ships." He also, however, suffers from the delusion of suspecting his chance visitors of being "the damned pirates" that have undone him, with the result that his monomania breaks out into maniacal tendencies. The next madman is a victim of phrenitis;

the immediate cause of his insanity is jealousy, and he spends the greater part of his time raving at the visitors, suspecting each in turn of having seduced his wife. The last of the three madmen has no trace of the choleric humor in him; he is a slightly drawn melancholic, whose phlegmatic qualities tend to make him more a fool than anything else. In *Northward Ho,* Dekker was to show comparatively greater restraint in his delineation of the two mad folk, perhaps because the emphasis of the scene is upon the trick played against Bellamont rather than upon the mad folk themselves. The bawd, the first of the two mad folk, insists that she is a virgin, and denies, without provocation, that she has ever been to Bridewell. She suffers from what would today be called dementia praecox, as is evidenced by her delusions that are combined with a persecution complex. The musician, on the other hand, is the victim of an abnormal and apparently unrequited love affair; his present symptoms are a penchant for talking in Italian and for making rather ghastly puns. The behavior of neither the bawd nor the musician is extreme; Dekker seems to have added nothing more than what he may have actually observed at Bethlehem. Furthermore, we already know that in 1557 Bethlehem Hospital was placed under the management of Bridewell, where persons guilty of immorality were confined; also, according to O'Donoghue, demented persons were occasionally transferred from Bridewell and accepted at Bethlehem, usually as charity patients. The bawd in *Northward Ho,* therefore, may very well have been an honestly reported sketch of a demented woman who, as her persistent denials suggest, had until recently been confined at Bridewell.

The madmen in Webster's *Duchess of Malfi* appear both too stereotyped in behavior and too well integrated with the tragic mood of the scene depicting the duchess's death to offer any sound information upon the actual behavior of the mad folk at Bethlehem; they are delineated as accessories to tragedy rather than as genuine symptomatic studies. Fletcher, however, in *The Pilgrim,* brings Bedlam directly to the stage with no other purpose than to exploit the inherent theatrical value of the inmates. Indeed, Fletcher's madmen, although they may be less honestly delineated than Dekker's, are more representative in the scope of their behavior than those of any other Jacobean playwright. There is, first of all, a "malt-mad" Englishman, clamoring for drink, who becomes sharply indignant when he is rebuked by the keeper. Next enters a "she-fool," described as being as "lecherous as a she-ferret"; her sexual mania is that of the moronic mind incapable of imposing self-restraint upon the predominant organic impulses. Fletcher's most interesting study, however, is the apparently discreet scholar, a young man of soundest intellect, indeed so discreet that he is about to receive his release papers; but a chance incident awakens the alternative ego and, with it, the inherent delusion that he is Neptune, the sea god, riding "upon a dolphin's back."

Fletcher, apparently, was not satisfied with only one scene of Bedlamites. A master of stage device, he undoubtedly felt that mad folk of this type were sufficiently effective to warrant an encore; consequently, later in the play, he brings back the Bedlamites, adding two more, a parson and a mad Welshman. Of these two, the Welshman is much the more distinctive; choleric by nature, he suffers from phrenitis, which is typically characterized by chronically impulsive, rather than inherent, delusions—in particular, by his prompt but mistaken assumption that the other inmates are "the devils, I know thee by thy tails."

What, then, can we say that the actual Bedlamite of the hospital was like? Was he, as a rule, as entertaining as Fletcher, in the early seventeenth century, and Ward, some eighty years later, would have us believe? Or was he as comparatively uninteresting as Dekker's musician and bawd appear to be? If we remove journalistic and theatrical trimmings, as Dekker has apparently done in *Northward*

Ho, and if we accept the fact that melancholy without adustion (the sudden combustion of the humor) was considered the most common Elizabethan mental disorder, we shall probably find that the average, or even slightly above average, Bedlamite was not highly interesting; but neither, for that matter, is the average monkey in the zoo. Every show has its individual stars, and undoubtedly "the show of Bethlehem" was no exception. If the average inmates, such as those suffering from the various depressive forms of melancholia, were unalluring to the Jacobean visitor, there were certainly a few Bedlamites who justified making the trip to Bedlam in addition to paying the probable admission fee. Fortunately, also, as far as entertainment was concerned, the "stars" were most likely those who were destined to remain longest in the hospital; they were, for example, victims of phrenitis that persisted until they became chronic maniacs; sufferers, also, from the more aggravated forms of melancholia, such as delusional insanity,[43] which by Jacobean interpretation resulted from adustion of the humor; and, finally, victims of extreme forms of mania who, although they had small hope of cure, had to be confined in order to avoid, as Lupton phrased it, "further and more desperate Inconveniences." Therefore, although patients with various depressive and comparatively uninteresting forms of melancholia were probably in the majority, there undoubtedly were, as the drama of the period attests, a number of psychotics to whose behavior Bethlehem owed its fame as a place of extraordinary amusement.

Also, it is well to remember that the inmates of old Bethlehem, unlike inmates of a modern asylum, were constantly agitated not only by the disconcerting conditions imposed by the poor management of the hospital, but also by the visitors themselves. Undoubtedly, the mad folk were often subjected to goading and, when this practice may not have sufficed, they were sometimes plied with liquor.[44] Consequently, it is not difficult to believe that the psychotic behavior of many of the mad folk was rendered on occasions much more abnormal than that which the visitor might expect to find in a similar institution today.

VII

Undoubtedly, as we have seen, there was often rather spectacular entertainment at the hospital. But what was the method of visiting? In the three Jacobean plays in which Bethlehem Hospital is used as the setting of one or more scenes,[45] the mad folk are brought into the "parlour" in order to entertain the visitors. This procedure undoubtedly was a necessary stage convention; more likely, upon an actual visit, the Jacobean visitor walked the "long entry," peeping into the cells as he passed. One hundred years later, upon the authority of both Brown and Ward, all the inmates except those with the mildest cases, who were occasionally granted "liberty of the Gallery," were, one by one, visited at the doors of their cells. Without a doubt this procedure of simply visiting the cells was the usual practice in old Bethlehem, a practice that is at least suggested in *Northward Ho* when Full-moone, having departed to look after the "unruly tenants," who are not permitted the liberty of the "parlour," is later joined by several of the visitors. Certainly, furthermore, if we are to believe "the cryings, screechings, roarings," and "shaking of chaines" reported by Lupton, it would have been a very unwise steward who would turn the more violent of his charges loose.

In *The Honest Whore,* Part I, Father Anselmo, the master of Bethlehem, advises the visitors:

Others again we have like hungry lions,
Fierce as wild-bulls, untameable as flies,
And these have oftentimes from strangers' sides
Snatched rapiers suddenly . . .
Whom if you'll see, you must be weaponless.[46]

The visitor, consequently, upon entering the hospital seems to have been obliged to leave his sword in safe custody, probably with the porter, before being admitted to the wards.

As the Jacobean visitor, therefore, having disposed of his sword, strolled through the "long entry," peeping here and there into a cell, he was undoubtedly aware of the physical discomfort of the unfortunate inmates. Straw was the only bedding permitted; also, no fires, even in wintertime, were permitted in the cells. Dekker and Webster in *Northward Ho,* for example, made a rather convincing documentary point of this condition in the incident in which Full-moone, the keeper, must refuse wood and coal for a fire, but has no objection to the request that Bellamont's straw be "fresh and sweet." Even a hundred years later, despite the fact that beds had supposedly been introduced into the new hospital at Moorfields, Brown, upon visiting Bethlehem, reported that the lunatics were confined "to straw, small drink, and flogging." If we consider the comparative poverty of old Bethlehem, a condition that led to slender and irregular meals and oftentimes to near starvation, if we consider also the harsh treatment and floggings to which the inmates were reportedly subjected, and then add the discomfort of straw for bedding and of cold winter mornings without a particle of heat, we must conclude that probably only sheer will power, abetted by the hope of escape, led to the eventual recovery of a good many of the curable patients.

There were probably, as we noted earlier, ten cells each in the north and the south wings of the hospital; the twenty-first on the ground floor, as reported in the muniment book in 1632, was quite possibly one of those small apartments that had originally replaced the old church at the rear of the rectangle. It is likely, therefore, that the visitor was confronted by patients with milder cases of insanity, perhaps dementia victims and other melancholics, in one wing, and by maniacs in the other. This supposition is supported by the disposition of the mad folk in Alibius's madhouse, which is the setting of the subplot in Middleton's *The Changeling* and which may very likely, for reasons that will be discussed in the next chapter, have been a satire upon Bethlehem itself. In *The Changeling*, the steward's responsibility of keeping order among the mad folk is more than enough for one man, but is made somewhat easier by the fact that the fools are kept in the ward to one side of the stage and the madmen in the ward to the other side. This disposition of the insane not only suggests a direct knowledge on the author's part of the separated wards of Bethlehem Hospital, but conversely indicates that the mad folk at Bethlehem were similarly segregated.

VIII

The general confusion reported by Lupton may at times have been true of old Bethlehem. Indeed, if we call to mind the apparently meager and irregular diet, the unheated cells, and the straw for bedding, we may readily believe that the inmates upon occasions vociferously objected to both their treatment and their surroundings. Diet, of course, was considered a basic treatment of victims of melancholia by both Bright and Burton. As a method of treatment at old Bethlehem Hospital, however, it appears to have been more or less nonexistent; likewise, the "refreshing entertainment" and "music" that Bartholomew de Glanville had recommended more than three centuries earlier are never mentioned by a contemporary author as being practiced at the hospital. On the other hand, from the evidence in Jacobean drama, whipping and the dark room seem to have been the two chief methods of treatment. The Sweeper, in *The Honest Whore*, for example, specifically claims that, having once been a "mad wag here" himself, he was lashed by Father Anselmo, keeper of the hospital, into his "right mind again." Shakespeare and Marston, both in turn, mention whipping as a cure for madness. In *The Pilgrim*, Alphonso is pronounced by the master of the hospital "dog-mad . . . Very far mad, and whips will scant recover you." Nevertheless, even though whipping had since ancient times been considered an accepted method of eradicating the "devil sickness," it is hard to believe that any of the mad folk at the hospital were actually cured by a treatment that modern psychiatry considers both detrimental and outrageous.

Whipping, moreover, was not always restricted to a means of treatment. This type of castigation, particularly at Bethlehem Hospital, appears to have become equally a method of controlling the unruly patients. Father Anselmo of *The Honest Whore,* for example, advises the visitors that the inmates must be "whipped for their unruliness." In *The Changeling,* the steward Lollio threatens the pseudomadman Franciscus with a whipping, not as treatment, but in order to restrain the latter's histrionic outbursts.

As for the dark room, I have already referred to passages from *As You Like It, Twelfth Night,* and Dekker's *Westward Ho* that prove the popularity of the dark room as a means of treatment. Marston makes a similar allusion to this type of treatment in *What You Will.* A somewhat more informative statement is found in Massinger's *A New Way To Pay Old Debts;* Justice Greedy suggests that Overreach be carried to "Bedlam"; the parson Willdo, who is a little more specific, advises a "dark room" and "try what art can do for his recovery."

There are, however, instances in drama of better treatment than whipping and the dark room; but they are comparatively few and hardly to be considered typical. Both King Lear and Ford's Meleander are restored to sanity by music. It should be noted, however, that in both these cases the circumstances are considerably refined: the patient is noble-born; the doctor is a private court physician; and, in each instance, the highly romantic mood of the play adapts itself to theory rather than to contemporary Jacobean practice. Consequently, the methods that are employed are idealized rather than documentary. Music could have served for kings and statesmen;

but whipping, a dark room, and chains were, by all outward appearances, considered sufficient for the inmates of Bethlehem Hospital.

John Gerarde published his book called *Herbals* in 1597; this was a complete compendium of pharmaceutical cures for insanity, many of them plucked from Dioscorides and Galen; rhubarb, wild thyme, black hellebore, and scarlet oak are only a few of the herbs that the author recommended. Later, the Jacobean court physician, Sir Theodore de Mayerne, prescribed compounds of herbs, but, as Dr. Tuke suggests, perhaps more benefit was acquired from the mental occupation of collecting the herbs than from the actual application. Although, for one example, Meleander in Ford's *Lover's Melancholy* is prescribed a drink compounded of herbs, there is no direct mention of such a practice at Bethlehem; nor is there any mention of bleeding the patients, another method practiced by Sir Theodore.

Despite the fact that we can hardly approve of the medical treatment of the inmates, the hospital in Jacobean times seems to have accepted, as a rule, only patients that were considered curable. This was quite definitely the practice, as we learn from John Strype,[47] at the new hospital immediately following the transfer in 1676 to Moorfields. Furthermore, Jacobean drama frequently testifies to the fact that the majority of confined inmates were not only curable, but eventually cured. Lollio, in *The Changeling,* for example, observes to the keeper's wife, Isabella: "You can cure fools and madmen faster than we."[48] On the other hand, as Lupton intimates, there were probably a small number of incurables confined to the hospital; but his statement, which reads "It's thought many are kept here, not so much in hope of recovery, as to keepe them from further and more desperate Inconveniences,"[49] clearly implies that acceptance of incurables was an exception and not the general policy of the hospital. How, then, if whipping and confinement to a dark room were the chief methods of treatment, were the majority of inmates expected to recover sufficiently to regain their liberties from the hospital? The chances are that whipping was reserved primarily for the more violent patients and that those with milder cases acquired some benefit from the quiet environment afforded by the dark-room treatment and probably greater benefit from the normal processes of nature.[50]

Thus far we have considered the medieval beliefs concerning insanity with particular emphasis upon the types of treatment; the foundation and the history of old Bethlehem Hospital at Bishops Gate Without; and the hospital in Jacobean times, with special consideration of the potential entertainment value of the inmates. What, then, was the particular reason that prompted at least five playwrights—Dekker, Webster, Fletcher, Middleton (or Rowley), and Ford—to reproduce the Bedlamites of the hospital directly upon the stage? Is it possible, for example, as Dr. Walsh suggested, that Bethlehem was actually taking away business from the theaters?[51] The chances are that the popularity of Bethlehem as a place of amusement did not noticeably interfere with the public's attendance at the theaters; the "show of Bethlehem," like our modern zoos, was something to be seen once or twice a year perhaps, but hardly, unless the particular person had a peculiar mania for such amusement, as a regular or weekly habit. The public theaters, of which there were several, appear to have introduced a new play every two weeks and to have rotated the shows of the repertory almost daily; the performance at Bethlehem, where personnel remained comparatively static, was probably, on the other hand, much the same, depending slightly upon variations of temperament, throughout any given quarter of the year. Such professionally minded playwrights as Dekker and Fletcher were, consequently, probably not prompted to employ scenes of Bedlamites by any necessity of winning back customers from the hospital, but rather by the fact that antics of mad folk, if embellished, were particularly suitable to the stage. In a drama peculiarly marked by showmanship and stage devices, nothing could have been better in tune with the excessive theatrical temperament than the uninhibited and carefully embellished symptoms of a few well-chosen Bedlamites. This, then, I take simply enough to have been the chief reason for the repeated reproduction of the hospital and its inmates on the stage; the lunatics offered, in brief, better and more spectacular entertainment on the stage, where selection and exaggeration were possible, than they did at Bethlehem Hospital.

2

In turning to the theatrical presentation of group madness, we should approach the study with two major points in mind: first, the playwright's artistic justification, if any, in the reproduction of Bedlamites, or group madness, upon the stage; second, the Bedlamites themselves as distinctive examples of the general extravagance of the period. From these considerations we can perhaps draw a reasonable estimate not only of the theatrical effectiveness, but also of the literary merits of the playwright's use of symptomatic madness, which was, as already indicated, a topic of recurrent importance in the Jacobean drama.

I

"How all?" asks the Sweeper in *The Honest Whore;* "why, if all the mad folk . . . should come hither, there would not be left ten men in the city."

"Few gentlemen or courtiers here, ha?" responds the Duke, inquiringly.

"O yes," replies the Sweeper, "abundance, abundance! lands no sooner fall into their hands but straight they run out a' their wits . . . Farmers' sons come hither like geese . . . and when they ha' sold all their corn-fields, here they sit and pick their straws." He further declares that women are "madder than March hares," and as for lawyers!—"we dare not let a lawyer come in, for he'll make 'em mad faster than we can recover 'em."[1]

The satiric implications are obvious; as mediums of satire these comments by the Sweeper of Bethlehem Hospital, which for the sake of the play is conveniently transposed to Milan, both illustrate and help to explain the playwright's artistic justification for introducing scenes of group madness into his drama. If his public demanded mad folk, the playwright, in so far as he was an artist, at least sought to justify the use of them. A display of madness, portraying symptoms that had no connection with plot or character development, was not in itself sufficient justification. Consequently, for the larger part, the Bedlamites in Jacobean drama were made either the instruments or the butts of the playwright's satire. Not only, therefore, were the grotesque and extravagant demands of the public amply satisfied, but also, by applying meaning and consequent significance to the symptomatic study, the playwright was able to preserve, to some extent at least, his own creative integrity.

In order to understand more fully the use of Bedlamites as butts of satire, let us turn back to the Sweeper. The Duke is an inquisitive fellow; he has inquired concerning the length of time necessary for the cure of mad folk. The Sweeper, who himself allegedly was once whipped to his senses, is only too ready to oblige; he observes that it's "according to the quantity of the moon . . . An alderman's son will be mad a great while . . . a whore will hardly come to her wits again," and as for a Puritan, poor fellow! "there's no hope of him, unless he may pull down the steeple, and hang himself i' the bell-ropes." All of this is good satire, and the more so since it does not invite animosity. By stressing the use of commonly laughed-at mad folk as the butts of the Sweeper's satire, Dekker removes much of the sting from what is actually his own personal criticism; significantly, moreover, if we call to mind the playwright's natural prejudice, the climax of the satire is directed against the uncompromising priggishness of the Puritans.

After the Sweeper's pungent criticisms, the Bedlamites are brought on the stage, and are used both as forcible mediums of theatricality and as butts or instruments of satire. The first, the monomaniac referred to in Chapter I, is reported to have been a grave and wealthy citizen, but has since lost all his wealth at sea. As a Bedlamite he is habitually draped in a net; he explains: "Dost not see, fool, there's a fresh salmon in 't . . . I am fishing here for five ships . . . but I'll break some of your necks an I catch you in my clutches." He shortly quiets down for the moment, mistakes the courtier Pioratto for his eldest son, and astutely observes, "I made him a scholar and he made himself a fool." After this instrumental use of satire, the onetime merchant reverts to what apparently obsesses him. "See, see, see, the Turk's galleys are fighting with my ships! . . . I am undone! . . . You are the damned pirates have undone me: You are, by the Lord, you are, you are!" At this point Father Anselmo must step out of hiding to prevent violence; he succeeds only by the promise of meat—to which the madman, confirming the probability of an irregular diet at Bethlehem, replies: "Ay, ay, pray do . . . these are my ribs . . . see how my guts come out! These are my red guts, my very red guts, oh, oh!" He is carted off, and it is under this circumstance that Anselmo advises that his lunatics must be "whipped for their unruliness," a procedure that seems to have been, as I have indicated, a regular practice at Bethlehem.

Before Bellafront, the converted whore, appears, rambling incoherently, but actually only pretending madness, Dekker introduces two more Bedlamites. Their act, though brief, is certainly not anticlimax; that unenviable distinction is reserved for the heroine Bellafront, for she is quite definitely miscast in a madhouse. Indeed, this incongruity confirms my belief that Dekker very deliberately contrived the particular setting that he might bring Bedlam in the year 1604 directly and for the first time to the English stage.

The slapstick antics of the second and third madmen undoubtedly incited a response from the Jacobean midriff. One of them, who is obsessed by the idea that his wife has had recourse to adultery, raves vituperatively at the Duke and his company, for he seems to suspect any young gallant. Having for the moment exhausted his invectives, he turns somewhat wearily to his companion, requests a bowl of porridge, then "flap-dragon." When the third madman fails to comply, the victim of phrenitis commits assault and battery upon him, an excess that was probably an exaggeration of anything that Dekker had witnessed at the hospital. His companion, now prostrate, thinks himself dead and cries out, "I am slain! ring out the bell!" Anselmo must humor him; he advises his servants to "bury him, for he's dead." To this, as he is being carried off the stage, the make-believe, but unabashed, corpse retorts: "Indeed, I am dead; put me, I pray, into a good pit-hole."

Considerably less spectacular, but not without evident satiric purpose, is Dekker's presentation of mad folk in *Northward Ho*. For no reason except to divert themselves, Bellamont, a dramatic poet who has never seen the inmates before, and his companions have stopped off at Bethlehem. The fact that this incident, having no essential relation to the plot, is an end in itself, attests to the popularity of Dekker's earlier mad folk in *The Honest Whore*. Fullmoone, the keeper, introduces two of the inmates to the visitors, and Bellamont, perhaps because he is a dramatic poet interested in gathering material, engages first the bawd, then the musician in conversation. The former, although brazenly professing that she is a virgin, is afflicted with a persecution complex and particularly with an aversion to young country gentlemen, who, despite the bawd's illusions of virginity, appear to have been the chief agents of her moral and mental degeneration. The musician is a little more exciting, but, like the bawd, apparently not overdrawn; he once fell mad for the love of an "Italian dwarf," fancies himself a gentleman, and has a habit of amusing himself and whoever will listen to him with puns. He is chiefly interesting as a satirical study of what Dekker might have thought of the contemporary courtier or young adventurer who had been to the continent for a few months and had returned home with a bagful of witticisms, a foreign tongue, and, as Dekker will have it, a mind that is temporarily demented.

Equally informative to the reader is Bellamont's narrow escape from confinement in the hospital. Undoubtedly, such pranks as his friends conceived were occasionally played at Bethlehem, and Dekker himself, as is suggested by his characterizing Bellamont as a dramatic poet, may have once been involved in a similar incident. In jest, but as part of a wager already made, the hero's friends declare him mad and easily convince Full-moone. Bellamont, despite his strenuous objections, is taken into custody and all but bedded down in straw; fortunately, since a "madman's" objections mean little, the joke is revealed.

Webster, in *The Duchess of Malfi,* introduces his madmen for quite a different dramatic purpose from that of Dekker; yet even this most tragic of tragic dramatists could not altogether escape the comic relief, however ironic it might be, that is inherent in Jacobean Bedlamites. When Ferdinand, who has already tortured his imprisoned sister, the duchess, with disclosure of the waxen images of her supposedly dead husband and children, subsequently promises to entertain her with madmen from "the common hospital," we are moved primarily by the terrifying irony of this suggestion. Webster is attaining his purpose: in brief, to build up an atmosphere symbolic of deranged mental terror in anticipation of the climactic episode in which the duchess and her protesting handmaid are murdered. Basically, this is the mood and specific purpose of Webster's mad folk; and, despite their caustic humor, they materially heighten the intense and macabre horror of a scene which, in all drama perhaps, is not surpassed for its atmosphere of preternatural terror.

The opening song by the madmen is an undisguised effort to paralyze the spine and nervous reflexes of the duchess. It begins:

O, let us howl some heavy note,
Some deadly dogged howl,
Sounding as from the threatening throat
Of beasts and fatal fowl![2]

All this, and more, is "sung to a dismal kind of music." The reader can well imagine the reserved awe and horror, and perhaps brutal satisfaction, of the Jacobean spectator.

However, once the madmen begin their conversation, they become less frightening. They are still not inconsistent with Webster's purpose of heightening the preternatural horror of the scene; but, conversely, they also provide the reader or the audience with a brief spell of comic relief, although of a definitely macabre sort. The madmen of *The Duchess of Malfi,* furthermore, all appear to suffer from deliberately devised forms of monomania; they are, on the whole, less flexible personalities than most of Dekker's and Fletcher's mad folk, largely because they are a little too profound and too consistent in their thought sequence; they lack the spontaneity and nicety of timing that permits a madman to shift, so to speak, with the wind. Each, in brief, suffers from a kind of mental fixity that prohibits more than a superficial response to external influences.

As already suggested, the humor of Webster's lunatics is ironically macabre; it consequently preserves, if it does not directly heighten, the mood of horror attained up to this point. But apparently Webster, having already subordinated the theatrical merits of his Bedlamites to an ulterior purpose, had an even more specific objective. The first madman, the astrologer, observes: "Doom's-day not come yet! I'll draw it nearer by a perspective . . . I cannot sleep; my pillow is stuffed with a litter of porcupines." Despite the comic undertone, there appears to be deliberate suggestiveness in this seemingly irrelevant statement: that is, death and the tortures of insomnia. Such suggestions, so closely identifying themselves with the mental anxiety of the duchess, must have been intended to cut deeply into her already irreparable state of shock. The next madman, likewise laboring under a mental obsession, reminds the duchess, who is already resigned to her death, of the tortures in hell, "where the devils are continually blowing up women's souls on hollow irons, and the fire never goes out." Straightway, the mad priest delivers what appears to be "the unkindest cut of all"; here, indeed, we become aware that these mad folk are merely the mouthpiece of the cruelly sadistic Ferdinand, himself mentally diseased. The priest, a fugitive lecher from his parish, exults: "I will lie with every woman in my parish the tenth night. I will tithe them over like haycocks." This suggestion of promiscuous adultery could have been intended only to add a smarting wound to the conscience of the already misunderstood and cruelly persecuted duchess, who has herself been charged with adultery.

The subsequent observations of Webster's madmen become less relevant to the situation and more generally satirical, but lack the spontaneous humor of Dekker's or even Fletcher's satire. Webster's forte was tragedy; his few attempts at comedy were apparently never very successful. Indeed, despite comments that out of context appear quaintly humorous, the madmen in *The Duchess* do not induce the reader to laugh; they hardly prompt a smile; they are much too formal, completely without repartee, and perhaps, under the intense circumstances, it is just as well anyway. The humor, if it may be called that, was meant to deepen the tragic effect.

If genuine humor, however, is lacking, the satire is nevertheless trenchant. The mad doctor, for example, imagines that his apothecary makes alum of his wife's urine, and sells it to the Puritans that have sore throats from overstraining. The same gentleman later concludes this comparatively formal "merry-making" by observing, "All the college may throw their hats at me: I have made a soap-boiler costive; it was my masterpiece." With this satiric stroke against the vain presumptions of the medical profession, Webster sends his lunatics into their madman's morris, and thus establishes the mood for the entrance of the chief executioner Bosola, disguised as an old man; at the sight of Bosola the distracted duchess cannot resist remarking: "Is he mad too?"

Together with *The Duchess of Malfi,* and, of course, with the exception of several of Shakespeare's plays, Middleton's *The Changeling* is often considered the outstanding tragedy of Jacobean drama. It is unquestionably a matter of coincidence that these two ranking tragedies of the period featured, each in its turn, a group portrayal of Bedlamites. On the other hand, it is a coincidence that never could have occurred in another period of drama; the vogue of group madness began and ended with the Jacobean period.

In *The Changeling,* as we know, the entire subplot is staged in an asylum called Alibius's Madhouse. If, as a work of literature, Middleton's great tragedy has succeeded, it has done so in spite of its mad scenes. On the other hand, as a contemporary spectacle, staged before a Jacobean audience, the mad folk undoubtedly contributed to the success of the play. So intense is the tragic action of *The Changeling* that some type of interspersion was essential; and by Jacobean theatrical standards nothing could have been more appropriate as a "second attraction" than the intrigues of persons confined to a madhouse.

O'Donoghue, in his history of Bethlehem Hospital,[3] suggests that Middleton (or Rowley) may have modeled the physician Alibius upon the notorious Dr. Crooke, who at the time of the production of *The Changeling* (1622–1624) had been master of Bethlehem Hospital some four or five years. The two men have definite similarities; Alibius, in the manner of Dr. Crooke, as revealed by the investigation of 1632 (to which I referred in Chapter 1), leaves the management of the asylum to his steward, while he himself, again like Dr. Crooke, who visited the hospital only "on quarter days," is occupied primarily with promoting business abroad. On the whole, though, Alibius and Lollio appear to be somewhat less disreputable characters than Crooke and his assistant, who, according to the investigation of the hospital in 1632, were charged with being wholesale extortionists and a year later were convicted and duly dismissed.[4] Nevertheless, Alibius, like Dr. Crooke, has no professional scruple against easy money. Lollio, lest he be slighted, demands and likewise receives a bribe from Pedro; he subsequently, as Dr. Crooke's steward apparently did, favors certain inmates according to their abilities to reimburse him. Meanwhile, Alibius, who, like Dr. Crooke, has a close connection at court, both readily accepts an offer to entertain the governor with his mad folk and comments, "We shall have coin and credit for our pains." Perhaps, as the play suggests, this could have been the beginning of a more profitable business; consequently, the physician Alibius, who admittedly "thrives by madmen and by fools," may well be a satire on Dr. Crooke when the latter was still a comparative novice; and, of course, in this case, Lollio is a satire upon the steward, with whom the author, as a visitor to the hospital, was almost undoubtedly better acquainted. Certainly, regardless of personalities, the madhouse scenes, as the author amply suggests, even making a veiled but fairly evident reference to the house as "Bedlam," appear to have been a satire upon Bethlehem Hospital. Moreover, no other asylum in London (if there were others) appears to have admitted public visitors.

Within the confines of the hospital the steward Lollio is supreme. He handles his charges with the versatility of a lion tamer. In the twinkling of an eye he can subdue an impending riot among the maddest mad folk; a moment later, still keeping up his conversation with the people on the stage, he is off again to pacify his "scholars" in the fools' ward. Despite the subsequent off-stage staccato cries of madmen, some imitating beasts, others birds, Lollio never quite loses his bearings. He sheds the confusion like so much rain water; he merely remarks, " 'Tis too much for one shepherd to govern two of these flocks . . . there will be some incurable mad of the one side, and very fools on the other."[5] The situation never appears to unnerve him; prompt in action, he is equally prompt in resignation. He can often, furthermore, pass off the confusion with a touch of humor, as he does on the occasion when the lunatics start clamoring for their dinner, a suggestion of the irregular diet with which Crooke and his steward were later charged: "You may hear what time of day it is," observes the resourceful Lollio; "the chimes of Bedlam goes."

Of the mad folk, Antonio, who acts the fool, and Franciscus, who acts the lunatic, are intended as burlesques of madmen. To the discerning eye, neither could pass as insane, simply because real madmen never follow carefully stereotyped blueprints of behavior; only when a man must feign madness does he resort to such evident conduct. Because Alibius, fearful lest someone among "the daily visitants" seduce his young wife, has warned Lollio to be on guard, the resourceful Antonio, who wishes to court Isabella, seeks admission as an inmate to the hospital. When Lollio inquires his name, Antonio replies, "He, he, he! well, I thank you, cousin; he, he, he!" A few obviously stereotyped answers such as this one apparently convince both Alibius and the steward that Antonio is unconditionally eligible for admission as one of the "scholars"; however, in fairness to their professional judgment, it should be added that a bribe is also instrumental in bringing them to this conclusion.

As an apparently intentional misrepresentation of a lunatic, Franciscus is a much more interesting study than Antonio. Feigning madness, he makes love to Isabella, while incoherently ranting in pseudoclassic rhetoric: "Hail, bright Titania! Why standest thou idle on these flowery banks? Oberon is dancing with his Dryades." All in all, his romantic delusions are more eloquent than those of any bona fide madman in the drama. Eventually, they become a little too eloquent and Lollio must threaten him with his whip. Franciscus cries: "O, hold thy hand, great Diomede! Thou feed'st thy horses well, they shall obey thee: Get up, Bucephalus kneels."[6] Consistently, the young gallant, confirming the rather obvious fact that he was intended only as a burlesque, kneels and is spared his whipping.

Perhaps the third of the three madhouse scenes most appealed to the Jacobean appetite for grotesque humor. Antonio is receiving instruction from the versatile Lollio in the fool's dance when Isabella enters. Observing the nimble Antonio, she is compelled to exclaim: "Hey, how he treads the air!" A few minutes later, the entire house of Bedlam is turned loose upon the stage, fools and madmen alike, each kind to its own dance. The "madman's morris," as in *The Duchess of Malfi,* appears to have been a highly popular climax, for it is evident that the audience preferred the abnormality of theatrical extravagance to dramatic moderation.

Middleton's lunatics were not the only example of group madness that distinguished the Jacobean stage in the early 1620's. In Fletcher's *The Pilgrim,* produced at the royal court in December 1621, the madmen are considerably more spectacular than those of *The Changeling.* During the early twenties of the seventeenth century, the rampant fever of "Bedlamitis" seems to have been near a peak of intensity. Middleton, or Rowley, went far out of his way to introduce scenes parodying Bethlehem Hospital in *The Changeling.* Fletcher in *The Pilgrim* adhered more closely to the story line of his plot; but the plot itself, as in Dekker's earlier *Honest Whore,* appears to have been deliberately contrived to include its madhouse scenes. There is also some historical evidence for the assumption that Bedlam was near the apex of its notoriety about this time. O'Donoghue in his history of Bethlehem Hospital tells us that King James, who had appointed the notorious Dr. Crooke as master in April 1619, not only claimed the privilege of legal guardianship of the institution, but in so doing made himself quite meddlesome. Indeed, according to O'Donoghue, he even imprisoned his attorney general Yelverton in 1620 for inserting a clause in the city charter granting the city the custody of Bethlehem. Between the King's patronage and the rumors concerning Dr. Crooke's negligence, there is good reason to believe that the hospital was enjoying more than its ordinary share of publicity.

Fletcher, in *The Pilgrim,* does far better than Middleton in organically justifying the Bedlam scenes. As already suggested, the "Madhouse," in which both the heroine and later her father are confined, is a setting that is essential to Fletcher's main plot, although the latter was almost undoubtedly contrived in order to include such a setting. Fletcher, however, makes the most of the opportunity. Madmen frolic on the stage as never before, but not without a brief warning of what is to come from the two keepers. One of them observes:

Carry Mad Bess some meat, she roars like thunder;
And tie the parson short, the moon's i' the full,
He has a thousand pigs in 's brains.[7]

With a sharp eye and a ready pen for satire, Fletcher quickly informs us that there is a justice, apparently a victim of delusional insanity, whom "the devil has possess'd . . . in the likeness of penal laws" and who is apparently serving warrants left and right among the other mad folk; whereupon, but quite incongruously, a "malt-mad" Englishman bolts onto the stage:

Give me some drink!

. . . .

Fill me a thousand pots, and froth 'em, froth 'em!
Down on your knees, you rogues, and pledge me roundly!

Rebuked by his keeper, the Englishman indignantly retorts:

A snuff, a snuff, a snuff
A lewd notorious snuff! give 't him again, boy.

Fletcher, unfortunately, cannot resist a habitual gravitation to the obscene. In bounces a she-fool, the one who is described as being "lecherous as a she-ferret." She observes, "Will you buss me, and tickle me, and make me laugh?" This alerts the hot-blooded Englishman, who immediately accosts her with the promise of getting her "with five fools." We are barely spared the fulfillment of this promise by the arrival of a third inmate of the house, the apparently very discreet scholar. Fletcher immediately illustrates the vivid realism with which he can sometimes treat his subject matter. Questioned by the master, the young scholar answers with such disarming discretion that his release papers are signed and he is about to leave the hospital, but mention is made of impending "stubborn weather." This remark apparently strikes a subconscious discord. The scholar's eyes are observed to "alter"; in a most reassuring manner, he advises:

Be not shaken,
Nor let the singing of the storm shoot through ye;

. . . .

Upon a dolphin's back I'll make all tremble,
For I am Neptune!

The "Napoleon complex" was as yet unheard of; but delusional insanity, as ancient in its dramatic appeal as Sophocles' *Ajax,* was something that Fletcher had probably observed at Bethlehem proper. Moreover, Fletcher's depiction of the scholar is particularly conducive to theatricality because of the contrast inherent in the dual personality.

Fletcher's first scene of madmen is almost a refreshing interlude. Even the plot, which is a loosely woven melodrama of bandits and misadventures, is given a more realistic and pronounced flavor. But Fletcher, aware of the theatrical appeal of well-delineated mad folk, was unwilling to restrict his lunatics to one scene, despite the fact that he has concentrated as much bedlam in it as exists in any other Jacobean play. In the third scene of Act IV, the madmen, a little less individualized, however, return with a gusto as free of inhibitions as a northeast hurricane:

Englishman: Bounce!
Clap her o' the starboard! bounce! top the can.

Scholar: Dead, ye dog, dead! do you quarrel in my kingdom?
Give me my trident!

Englishman: Bounce, 'twixt wind and water,
Loaden with mackerel! Oh, brave meat!

Scholar: My sea-horses!
I'll charge the northern wind, and break his bladder!

Parson: I'll sell my bells, before I be out-braved thus.

And with further threats of "I'll curse ye all! I'll excommunicate ye!" the parson enters into the argument with as much vigor as the best of them. We can well imagine the provocation that the parson and the scholar must have offered to the indelicate Jacobean sense of humor! The latter lunatic reminds us of what Burton in *The Anatomy of Melancholy* had recently written about scholars: their wits dry up, they go mad, or else they end up in the country "chatting with fools." The choleric Alphonso, merely a spectator up to this point, yet as sanguinely robust as any Jacobean, expresses the will of all: "Mad gallants, most admirable mad; I love their fancies." But this is not quite all; Fletcher climaxes the scene with a Welsh madman, who, as a butt of satire, is perhaps the masterpiece of the play. With native valiancy, he challenges all comers: "I'll beat thy face black as a blue clout," and a moment later, "Thou are the devils, I know thee by thy tails. . . I will pig thy bums full of bullets." To these comments, Alphonso is compelled to remark, "This is the rarest rascal!"

The theatricality of Fletcher's mad folk, particularly of the scholar, is quite evident. But Alphonso's appreciative remark pertaining to the Welshman suggests that the Jacobean audience, although interested primarily in the theatricality of the Bedlamites, was not insensitive to the satire that underlay many of the studies. Indeed, the satirical implications that are a part of the foregoing studies not only contribute meaning and significance, but also enhance the theatrical appeal because the satire, as popular satire should be, is almost invariably universalized. The individual madman, as we have noted, serves only as the immediate butt of the satire; through him, whether he is Fletcher's Welshman, Dekker's merchant, or Webster's doctor, entire professions or classes of people are ridiculed. As a result, the satire, while first providing the Bedlamite with a degree of literary merit, also gave proportionally greater scope and emphasis to the spectacle; not one unfortunate individual, but a whole class of them was made the subject of derisive display, inseparable from the theatricality itself. With this point in mind, we can be quite certain that not only the self-gratification but also the entertainment and the applause of the Jacobean audience were correspondingly multiplied, simply because it was laughing not at one individual, but at many.

II

Before making a final conclusion as to the topic of this chapter, we shall consider briefly a second type of symptomatic portrayal. Even though the foregoing scenes of group madness are a distinct kind, they are not the only instances in Jacobean drama in which the playwright exploited strictly symptomatic madness, that is, the spectacle of madness without a careful analysis of its causes.

Several individual and isolated portrayals of this class are akin to the presentations of group madness in so far as the causes of insanity are either, like those of several Bedlamites, merely reported or, at worst, unjustified. In marked contrast to the pathological studies, which will be discussed later, the playwright was concerned almost entirely with the symptomatic portrayal of madness and its theatrical potentiality. That we may better evaluate the different dramatic uses of madness, it is well to consider a few of these characters.

In *The Witch of Edmonton,* produced about 1623, Dekker and his collaborators were concerned primarily with witchcraft; but there is one incident in this play that, considered by itself, is a symptomatic display of madness and not a psychological study of either witchcraft or insanity, namely, the brief appearance of Ann Ratcliffe. She is, however, given just enough case history to arouse a momentary pang of sympathy in the reader. For a trivial and meaningless offense, Mother Sawyer has, with the help of the devil, turned the poor girl out of her wits.[8] But this is merely reported, and when we first meet Ann, she is already insane and escorted by her husband; she immediately blabs idiotic snatches: "See, see, see! The man i' th' moon has built a new windmill. . . Prithee, let me scratch thy face." At this point the black Dog, incarnation of the devil, rubs himself against her leg; Ann, already demented, is straightway stricken with climactic fury; as Mother Sawyer vengefully gloats, the maniacal girl tears herself loose from her husband, runs off stage, and dashes out her brains. Her appearance is brief, but memorable. The circumstances leading to Ann's madness are neither fully nor pathologically explained; nevertheless, as an innocent victim she commands our sympathy; but, what may have been more important to the Jacobean, she certainly reproduces the atmosphere of bedlam, however briefly, at a very high intensity upon the stage.

Ben Jonson depicted almost every type of eccentric personality; indeed, many of them, if not the majority, are embodiments of one of the humors of which Jonson's psychological theory was compounded. Never again, until the time of Dickens, did an author reproduce such an unforgettable ensemblage of eccentrics, rogues, and prospective cutthroats. Loosely, one might consider half of Jonson's comic characters plausible candidates for a cell in Bethlehem if they did not land in jail first; actually, however, Trouble-All in *Bartholomew Fair* is probably Jonson's only character that the master intended as a "madman." The other eccentrics, with the possible exceptions of Zeal-of-the-Land and Morose, were undoubtedly felt to be quite sane enough by contemporary standards.

Trouble-All's case history is rather slight. He was once a justice of the peace; but having lost his office, and troubled by his "ignominious deposition," he has very conveniently, as far as the play is concerned, gone mad. We are introduced to him in the fourth act and immediately learn that he haunts Bartholomew Fair yearly and will permit nobody, including himself, to perform any action without a warrant from Justice Overdo. If not altogether convincing, Trouble-All is at least a very comic study of a monomaniac. From beginning to end he harps upon warrants; moreover, he misinterprets the obsession under which he labors as his sacred and perfectly sincere mission in life.

Trouble-All: There must be a warrant had, believe it.
Winwife: For what?
Trouble-All: For whatsoever it is, anythinge indeed,
no matter what.

"No matter what" is specifically correct. He not only succeeds in freeing several prisoners from the stocks because of his insistence upon a "warrant," but according to his unflinching philosophy warrants must be had for everything else, even for spending one's money. Jonson, of course, is satirizing the paucity of mental ingenuity among lawyers and justices of the peace, whose professional thinking had, even at that early date, long been restricted by the narrow limits of legal phraseology and procedure. The Jacobeans, who were certain to enjoy the spectacle of Trouble-All's madness, were probably for the most part experienced enough with beadles, constables, and judges to comprehend and appreciate the incisive implications of Jonson's satire.

Perhaps no other Jacobean playwright tried more persistently to interpret the Jonsonian theory of humors than did John Fletcher, if we except the comic master himself. But, by contrast to Jonson's characters, those of Fletcher, and particularly those who suffer from the excess of some humor, are almost invariably superficial; but, nevertheless, they are often scintillating. They are unweighted by any serious philosophy; their troubles exist largely in their imaginations; and, furthermore, many of them appear to take personal pleasure in the notoriety that is gained by eccentric behavior. Whereas Jonson's characters personify the more serious foibles of human nature, those of Fletcher embody ephemeral whims for the most part. It is for this reason that his eccentrics, unlike Jonson's, are almost always curable; despite Fletcher's intention, most of them are not strictly humor characters.

Among the most entertaining of Fletcher's comic eccentrics are his madmen, not only those already discussed, the Bedlamites from *The Pilgrim,* but two characters who are functionally necessary to the plots in which they appear—the Passionate Lord and Shatil-lion. Only in the comic sense, moreover, are they studies in case history, for neither of them has a good reason to be mad in the first place. The madness of the Passionate Lord in the comedy entitled *The Nice Valour,* a play that some critics assign in part to Beaumont, results, for example, merely from a fabricated whim. As he is a much more interesting person when mad than when in his right mind, he seems, furthermore, to support Fletcher's own hypothesis[9] that insanity was as much a fashion of the times as a disease. It was certain, of course, to attain considerable notoriety.

There being no cause for the Passionate Lord's madness, he at least suffers the illusion that his Lady has spurned him. She, who loves him dearly, must finally resort to disguising herself as the love god Cupid in order to "draw all his wild passions to one point only." But the Passionate Lord is not to be easily cajoled out of his various humors. On the contrary, the hero's madness is carefully provided with immunity against its normal cure, which is, of course, a reconciliation with his Lady. He has completely lost his ability to identify persons, including his ladylove, and haunts the palace in a mentally stupefied condition. Ironically, without explanation, he mistakes the courtier La Nove for his Lady and calls him "thou fairest, yet the falsest woman, that ever broke man's heartstrings." Nor, as already suggested, does the Passionate Lord suffer from love-melancholy only; he also, by the playwright's contrivance, suffers from all the other humors. Shamont, another courtier, who is unable to endure any absurdity, calls him "thou four elements ill-brewed." In using the word "ill-brewed," Shamont has, perhaps unintentionally, employed the *double-entendre*. The Passionate Lord may run "through all the passions of mankind, and shift 'em strangely," but the playwright, except as pure burlesque, has demanded too much of one man.

For more than half the play the Passionate Lord is in a very despondent mood—"untrussed, untailored." However, we are suddenly reminded that "the tail of his melancholy is always the head of his anger." Although unconvincing as a study in insanity, the Passionate Lord is an excellent vaudevillian, and his anger is certainly more entertaining than his love-melancholy. He calls violently from off stage for his food: "My maintenance, rascals!" A moment later he rushes furiously onto the stage, truncheon in hand; without warrant he vents his rage on Lapet:

A curse upon thee for a slave!

. . . .

Death, hell, fiends, and darkness!
I will thrash thy mangy carcass.[10]

He then ignores Lapet's affable "Oh, sweet sir!" and beats him to
the ground.

At the beginning of the fifth act we find our pardoxical madman
in "a violent fit of mirth." His love-melancholy and choler are mag-
ically forgotten; the author instead has put the sanguine humor to
work, and as a result the Passionate Lord sings as hilarious a re-
frain of robust nonsense as ever tickled a Jacobean's ear. The reader
of the play now has a right to expect some kind of exhibition of the
fourth humor, which is phlegm; he has been informed more than
once that the hero's repertoire includes all the four "elements"; but,
of course, Fletcher (or Beaumont, or both) had better theatrical
sense than to include a display of phlegm, which, being a negative
humor, rarely led to spectacular episodes. As a study in madness
the Passionate Lord deserves no place in literature; but as a
theatrical device he offers further and fairly convincing testimony
to the fact that extravagant exhibition, not dramatic authenticity,
was the major element of entertainment most desired by the
Jacobean audience.

If the Passionate Lord had no apparent cause for his madness,
Shatillion in *The Noble Gentleman,* which quite possibly was the
last play written by Fletcher, has only the slightest reason; his
mistress, we are told, has given him "a coy denial." Although
Shatillion's humors are confined to only one type of madness, love-
melancholy, he appears to be an even more versatile showman, certainly a more sensitive artist, than the Passionate Lord. Where
the latter ultimately resorted to excessive outbursts of anger and
then of mirth, Shatillion can make love-melancholy, unabetted by
the other humors, worth the price of admission itself. He is an

artist within his field; as a satire upon a lovelorn courtier, there is hardly anything better in Jacobean drama. However, like the Passionate Lord, he must not be mistaken for a study in madness; Shatillion is purely a burlesque; the chief difference is that as burlesque he is a much more subtle study than is his predecessor.

Shatillion, like the Passionate Lord, has conveniently lost all sense of recognition; the normal human capability of identifying persons and circumstances has been split from a mind that is otherwise active and seemingly logical, although its logic is invariably based on false premises. Shocked by the "coy denial" of his mistress, Shatillion has become stubbornly enveloped in a detached world of inverted judgments. It is this unparalleled flair for misinterpreting reality, abetted by an abiding sense of chivalry, that chiefly distinguishes him as a showman.

The fertile, if misguided, imagination of Shatillion is apparent from the time of his first appearance. Jilted out of the normal use of his judgment, he imagines his sweetheart to be the heir apparent after the king and consequently imprisoned lest she marry Shatillion. His imagination has immediately taken a further step; as a consequence of the king's supposed imprisonment of his mistress, he suspects everybody of treason against his own life. This dilemma is accentuated by his failure to recognize both his mistress and his closest friends, whom he mistakes for agents of the king. Burton, quoting Montanus, had written: "One [type of melancholic] fears every man he meets . . . will kill him"; a little later, Burton added: "Some suspect treason."[11] As a result of such delusions and consequent irregularities in behavior, the ever-apprehensive Shatillion is fittingly described as "March-mad." What particularly distinguishes Shatillion, however, is his unquenchable loyalty to his king; if he misinterprets everything else, he never forgets his sworn allegiance to the king, even though he thinks the latter plots against his life. He entreats a favor, for example:

To see my Love, before that fatal stroke,
And publish to the world my Christian death,
And true obedience to the crown of France.[12]

Nor, when waylaid by "some twenty musketeers"—actually figments of his imagination—does he forget the stamp of valor expected of the courtier; he spurns the odds and, with debonair courage and drawn sword, marches to the attack.

Fittingly, in the end, this lovelorn courtier is restored to his senses, not by an ordinary process, but by physically tumbling the presumptuous Monsieur Mount-Marine, who has set himself up as a duke, from his throne. Thus, as Shatillion supposes, he has vindicated the authority of his king. As the foregoing incidents suggest, Shatillion is an exhibitionist, an unpredictable artist, who can occasionally approach comic grandeur while never quite disintegrating into ludicrous farce. As a satire upon a love-crazed courtier who instinctively could not forget his royal obligations, Shatillion is something more than a vehicle of theatricality; he is also the unwitting comic artist who, failing to observe the humor of his own behavior, invites the bulk of the laughter on himself.

Massinger, unlike Jonson and Fletcher, did not specialize almost exclusively in eccentric characterizations. Indeed, some critics characterize his works as "passionless," with the implication that he depended more upon plot construction than upon emotional display. This appraisal may be true of many of his plays, notably perhaps *The Maid of Honor,* upon which much of his fame as a perfectionist rests; but it certainly is not true of all of them, particularly of such tragedies as *The Unnatural Combat* and *The Virgin Martyr.* Nor is the epithet of "passionless" altogether fitting to his comedies. Even though most of the characters are delineated as comparatively normal human beings, Massinger was too professionally skilled to overlook the appeal of abnormality. Luke in *The City Madam* and Overreach in *A New Way To Pay Old*

Debts are testimony in themselves that Massinger depended, like his older contemporaries, upon one or more indisputably abnormal characters with which to motivate the machinery of his comic plots.

Overreach's madness is briefly discussed in this chapter because, as a case history, it does not appear sufficiently convincing for pathological interpretation. It is almost entirely a symptomatic study. The lack of proper pathological background results from the fact that the climactic insanity of the broken usurer, of the man who had once likened himself to the rock on which the "foaming billows" split, was almost undoubtedly an afterthought by the author. On the other hand, the fury of it certainly cannot be considered inconsistent. A turbulent character from the beginning, heedless of others' poverty, bent only upon their ruin, Overreach can hardly be expected to retire from the scene once the trick is turned against him; the reader expects a new crest of fury, but he is a little surprised that the hardened warrior, without previous suggestion or precedent, goes completely mad. His deed and his daughter lost, Overreach is momentarily stunned. "Confusion and ruin!" he cries. At this point it is proper that the man who had once likened himself to a rock should bellow in defiance and self-justification; but we expect him to do it halfway sanely; instead, in his own words, his "brain turns." Foiled in his attempt to kill his daughter, he threatens to make the "house a heap of ashes" and not to leave "one throat uncut." When he fails to obtain assistance, his fury mounts; he flourishes his sword and prepares to "fall to execution." Shortly, having been unexpectedly foiled by some invisible power, he imagines that he is confronted by "hangmen" and Furies; and his final sally, as the reader will recall, ends in utmost frustration with Overreach flat on the ground, while he foams at the mouth and bites the earth.

Overreach's madness may, as poetic justice, be well deserved, but pathologically it is ill-grounded. Massinger, as in most of his plays, has permitted his professional purpose to interfere with his dramatic aims. He has, so to speak, thrown Overreach, heretofore a genuine interpretation of a usurer, to the groundlings. The applause of his own audience, not that of aftertime, appears in general to have been the chief objective of the professional Jacobean playwright. To this theatrically sound rule, Massinger, despite the epithet of "passionless," was not an exception.

III

What, then, are the major characteristics of the preceding studies, which include the Bedlamites on the one hand and, on the other, individual examples of symptomatic madness? First of all, as I have noted, the playwrights in reproducing symptomatic studies almost invariably justified the theatrical abnormality of such depictions by making the mad folk the butts, and sometimes the instruments,[13] of satire; this justification is particularly obvious in the scenes depicting the actual Bedlamites, in which, as the reader has observed, lawyers, preachers, doctors, merchants, scholars, and overzealous lovers are, one after another, indirectly ridiculed through the exploitation of their demented colleagues as the butts of satire. Likewise, the individual portrayals of symptomatic madness, such as Trouble-All, are more often than not made the mediums through which certain broad types or professions of people are satirized. In summary, then, satire was the poet's artistic justification; it gave meaning and intelligence to his studies, and was particularly essential to the Bedlamite scenes, which otherwise would have no significance beyond the applause of the contemporary audience. Mere stereotypes of symptomatic abnormality may have sufficed for the less intellectual spectators; but the playwright, by the ingenuity of his satire, lost little and gained much; for, in addition to applying literary merit, the satire also enlarged the scope of the spectacle because, as has been previously stressed, it tended to universalize, as a rule, the object of the audience's derision.

Even though most of the preceding symptomatic reproductions are artistically justified by being made the butts, or occasionally the instruments, of satire, their primary purpose is certainly to provide the audience with spectacular entertainment. A playwright is not likely to introduce characters, such as the Bedlamites, who are irrelevant to the plot, for the subordinate purpose of ridiculing certain professions; on the other hand, the long-experienced Jacobean playwright was incessantly aware of the popularity of spectacle as a theatrical convention. Spectacle, then, regardless of the degree to which the satire tended to enlarge its scope, was both the chief motive and the chief characteristic of most of the mad-folk scenes that have been summarized in this chapter; if the popularity of Bethlehem Hospital was a direct influence upon the reproduction of mad folk upon the stage, this was so primarily because the grotesque and unexpected behavior of Bedlamites, particularly when elaborated upon, typified the theatrical extravagance that the Jacobean audience seems to have unflaggingly demanded of its playwrights. According to Bacon, it was the habit of King James and Buckingham "to love to do things unexpected"; and, according to Professor F. P. Wilson, this love of the unexpected not only influenced but also expressed the spirit of Jacobean romantic comedy.[14] As vehicles of spectacle and surprise that stressed, above all, the unpredictability of human behavior, the Bedlamites of Dekker and Fletcher, the climactic fury of Overreach, and the explosive and "ill-brewed" versatility of the Passionate Lord are strictly the homogeneous products of the Jacobean stage; they could not properly belong to any other period in English dramatic literature.

3

Whereas Bethlehem Hospital and its inmates had undoubtedly been the chief formulative influence upon the theatrical use of group madness and probably an indirect influence upon symptomatic studies as a whole, we must look elsewhere for the major influences that determined another and more prevalent dramatic type of madness. In contrast to the Bedlamites, who were presented to the audience primarily as spectacle, such pathological studies of insanity as Lear, Webster's Ferdinand and Cornelia, and Ford's Penthea offered not only spectacle, but also a comparatively comprehensive analysis of the perversities that their creators felt both underlie and, to a large extent, determine human behavior. In this respect, in the interpretation of what man thought about man, the carefully analyzed psychopathic studies of the Jacobean stage, together with the morally degenerate backgrounds against which they were depicted, are unusually informative to us because many of them reflect the Jacobean's psychological attitude toward the world in which he lived. These comparatively intricate studies, however, would probably not have been possible if Elizabethan pathological theories, reaching their full development by the end of the sixteenth century, had not been available to such playwrights as Shakespeare, Jonson, Webster, and, finally, to Ford.

I

Elizabethan mental pathology, in marked contrast to modern psychology, had its direct origins in classical times. The Greek physician Hippocrates, about 400 B.C., had speculated upon the four material liquids of the body—blood, phlegm, choler, and melancholy; he had particularly considered their influence upon physical disease, which, he concluded, resulted from the deficiency of the humor in one part of the body or from its surcharge in another part. Considerably later, about 170 A.D., Galen, the court physician to Marcus Aurelius, advanced the theory that these four humors were, by excess or deficiency, responsible not only for physical disease but also for the peculiarities of behavior. The mind, he said, might also be adversely affected by the vitiated condition of a humor. Galen's experimental psychology, the major premise of which was the theory that the humors directly affected human behavior, remained throughout medieval times the final, if not universally understood, authority in its field. Not until the Spanish physician Juan Huarte and the English doctor Timothy Bright published their works on the humor theories in 1580 and 1586, respectively, were the conclusions of Galen appreciably modernized.

First, however, in order more fully to comprehend Elizabethan mental pathology, we shall briefly consider the once-famous Elizabethan treatise on anatomy that was written, and published in 1548, by Dr. Thomas Vicary, surgeon-in-charge of St. Bartholomew's Hospital, London; this book was republished less than thirty years later, in 1577, as testimony to the authority in which it was then held, by Vicary's fellow surgeons.[1] Vicary's work does not discuss psychology; it is, on the contrary, concerned entirely with the anatomy and the functions of the human body. Where the anatomical functions, however, remained poorly understood, Vicary was compelled to make somewhat nebulous, but in his own age credible, deductions that eventually brought him to a discussion of the liquid "juices" and "superfluities," which are identified as the humors. A major responsibility of the liver, for example, was to drain the stomach of its "fermented juices"; they, in turn, united with the "spiritual blood," which had entered the liver through an artery from the head and upper regions. Combined, these two elements created nutritive blood, which, in its turn, was dispersed by the nutritive vein and its lesser tributaries through the body.[2] This functional operation, according to Vicary, must be in perfect balance in order to assure good health; he implied that an overabundance of nutritive blood within the liver, if it could not be adequately purged or discharged, would jeopardize the functional health of the body. But Vicary, although he directly mentions the humors, was not concerned with a psychological interpretation of them; had he been, he would have almost undoubtedly concurred with the theory of Bright, as set forth thirty-eight years later, that unnatural lust, regardless of physical disease, resulted from an overabundance of nutritive blood in the liver.

The gall bladder, Vicary concluded, was ordained "to receyve the cholerike superfluities" of the liver; and these, in turn, were dispersed to the stomach and guts to aid digestion.[3] Vicary again had implied the essentiality of perfect operational balance. If otherwise, if the "cholerike superfluities" should not be uniformly discharged from the gall bladder, we may conclude with Galen, Huarte, and Bright that the patient was very liable to suffer, through either excess or excrement, from the psychological effects of the choleric humor; this humor, moreover, once it was adust, was considered the instrument of the most violent passions of all.

In discussing the functional operations of the spleen and the lungs, Vicary continued to suggest the relation that existed between the anatomical functions of particular organs, on the one hand, and the psychopathic humor theory on the other, although he never explicitly tied the two theories together. The spleen, for example, received the "melancholious superfluities" from the liver; so far, in this function of intake, its operation corresponded to that of the gall bladder. The spleen, however, in Vicary's interpretation, did not discharge these superfluities; it apparently absorbed them.[4] Therefore, if we apply the functional theory of absorption rather than that of dispersion to the humor principles of Timothy Bright, we may sensibly conclude that the melancholic humor, unable by anatomical interpretation to be discharged from the spleen and, consequently, subject to unusual concentration, was upon sound medical premises felt to be the most readily disordered, and in that sense the most dangerous, of the Elizabethan humors. Indeed, partially as a result of the skepticism of the late 1590's, melancholy was soon to receive far and away the most discussion among the humors in the contemporary literature; and it is interesting to note that the widespread concern over melancholy had the apparent approbation of the medical profession.

The lungs, according to Vicary, not only were the seat of "Flegme,"[5] but they also purified the air which a person breathed, dispatched it to the heart in order to cool and refresh the latter, and then received the "superfluities that the harte putteth foorth with hys breathing."[6] The lungs were generally considered, although Bright himself makes no such direct statement, the seat of the phlegmatic humor; the implication of Vicary's functional interpretation was simply, as it was regarding the other vital functions just discussed, that a surplus—in this case, of the superfluities of the "harte's breathing"—would result in the corresponding humor, phlegm.

Vicary might be loosely termed the Elizabethan Hippocrates; Bright, on the other hand, both acknowledges and clearly indicates a direct debt to Galen and differs from him only on the one major issue wherein the English physician makes a clear-cut distinction between natural melancholy and the direct infliction of "the heavy hande of God," which he said might strike at the soul or human conscience regardless of pathological causes. More to our point, however, and generally consistent with the functional operations of the liver, gall bladder, spleen, and lungs, as they had been expounded by the surgeon Vicary, were Bright's basic, but somewhat more intricate, humor theories. Vicary, of course, had been concerned only with the anatomical functions of the body; Bright, in the famous *Treatise of Melancholie,* which both influenced and later closely represented the Elizabethan theory of humors, accepted, although with one or two notable variations, the functional anatomy of Vicary and, associating lust with the liver, melancholy with the spleen, choler with the gall bladder, expounded an almost purely psychological doctrine, the purpose of which was to explain as logically as he could the pathology of the humors and, particularly, that of melancholy. Bright's treatise constitutes the first substantial interpretation of the causes and symptoms of mental disease that was written by an Englishman; furthermore, in its scientific deductions, which were confined largely to contemporary medical interpretation, it was unquestionably a more concretely and professionally influential work than Burton's *Anatomy of Melancholy,* published thirty-five years later. Bright condensed the fragmentary knowledge of his times into a solid doctrine of humors; Burton compiled a highly readable encyclopedia of all the information regarding insanity that had ever been published, but his work is a masterpiece of anecdote, vernacular, and knowledge rather than of any sustained pathological conviction. In the section, for example, that deals with symptoms of melancholy, when Burton ultimately expresses doctrines upon which he can concur with sincerity rather than with a tone of amusement, his conclusions are, as he gladly informs us, those of Timothy Bright.[7]

What then, basically, were the principal humor theories of Bright's treatise, a work that was, and still is, considered the most representative thesis upon melancholy and insanity of the Elizabethan period? As a fundamental premise Bright, tacitly applying Vicary's principle of the necessity of perfect functional relation, explained the melancholic humor as resulting either from an excessive thickness of the grosser part of the blood or from the excrements of melancholic juices drawn from the liver, either of which conditions, if improperly purged by the spleen, would create dangerous fumes. Bright, of course, was primarily concerned with melancholy; but, in generalizing, he applied his theory of over-nourishment and excrement to all the humors. Bright goes on to become more specific, if no less hypothetical; once the melancholic humor, for example, had begun to corrupt and had failed to be properly purged, vapors would rise from the spleen to the brain and darken it with hideous and mistaken fantasies; from the brain, in turn, the disordered fancies would pass to the heart and cause fear, distrust, sadness, or despair.[8] At this point, of course, Bright had already made a necessary departure from any further dependence upon anatomical theory. Beyond both an early, but explicit, acknowledgment of the essentiality of functional balance and a recognition of the liver, spleen, and gall bladder as the "seats" of their respective humors, Bright seems to have owed little else to accepted Elizabethan anatomy. Once he had done with functional balance, his theories, as already indicated, belonged almost entirely to the field of psychology.

Bright, accepting the common opinion of his time, had, in the opening chapters of his treatise, stated that most foods, particularly meats, were composed of dangerous humors and had blamed over-eating or improper diet as the chief stimulator of the melancholic humor, which theoretically resulted, as we have observed, either from excess of nourishment to the blood's grosser part or from the putre-faction of the melancholic discharge of the liver. Once a humor became active, Bright further argued that it would distemper or dis-quiet the heart or cause misconceptions to the brain, or both, but implied that it was not as a rule sufficient in itself to arouse inor-dinate passions. According to Bright, an external cause was almost always necessary to incite the particular humor to one of its more severe passions, although the cause might often be slight or even misconceived.[9] In the case of choler, for example, the humor might ordinarily appear to be negative, but a misconceived offence would provoke a tempestuous outburst of anger, which could be particularly severe and lengthy if the disaffection were in the brain.[10] Melancholy, moreover, was characterized by the greatest variety of symptoms. These symptoms were determined by "the diversity of place" where the humor settled, such as the brain, spleen, heart, or stomach; or by the condition of the humor—natural, unnatural, or compounded; or by the nature of the external offense. Bright, however, makes clear one major exception to the general rule that an external offense was essential to stir inordinate passion. The melancholy humor, he concluded, was often sufficient in itself to cause a person to suffer mistaken fancies and delusions resulting in pronounced sorrow or fear; but, like the other humors, it required an outside offense to provoke a more severe and sometimes uncontrollable passion. As the sanguine humor was prompted to excessive mirth by "the wagging of a feather," likewise melancholy, wrote Bright, "doubleth its sorrow upon small occasion."

Unnatural melancholy, according to Bright, was "by an unproper speech" so called; it was, instead, a madness resulting from the combustion of *any* of the four natural humors "by excessive distemper of heat . . . into ashes." Such an "adustion" of the humor, leading to the most violent and often incurable passions, was considered by Bright and by most of his contemporaries to be prerequisite to actual insanity.

Melancholy, as every student of the Elizabethan period knows, was a constant topic of the contemporary literature. Among poets, Breton, Daniel, and Campion were perhaps particularly mindful of the pathology of melancholy; among pamphleteers, Nashe in *The Terrors of The Night* drew an acute picture of the terrifying apparitions of "fuming melancholy"; but the great majority of the allusions to melancholy, in addition to the comparatively more important pathological studies of insanity, are quite significantly found among the dramatists, particularly in the works of Marston, Shakespeare, Tourneur, Webster, and Ford. It was the playwright who was by nature and by the democratic circumstance of his profession closest to the emotional pulse beat of contemporary England; he, therefore, most honestly represented the Jacobean's psychological misgivings, which, in turn, are repeatedly reflected by his own professional interest in the pathology of mental disease. "What is man," the playwright seems to have asked, "and what is wrong with him?" As the drama of the period amply testifies, he found the pathological answer to this question in the theories of the humors and, especially, in those of melancholy.

If the allusions to melancholy in the poetry, journals, and drama of the period are many, it is the serious dramatic interpretations of psychopathic persons that betray the most extensive debt to the theories of melancholy and of insanity as they were promulgated by Bright. First of all, the frequency of these dramatic studies, beginning about 1601 and continuing through the creative period of Ford, indicates in itself a persistent and conscious interest in mental pathology, not only among the playwrights but also among the audiences, whose sentiments, after all, determined to a large extent the type of story and of character presented upon the stage. In the 1590's, by contrast, there had been much talk and literary speculation about melancholy, but actual dramatic presentations of insanity had remained comparatively rare and, when presented, they were usually awkwardly sketched. Secondly, a reasonably careful analysis of the Jacobean playwrights' pathological studies, particularly those of Shakespeare, Webster, Massinger, and Ford, indicates not only an interest in, but a professional knowledge of, contemporary psychiatric theory. A natural humor, usually melancholy or choler, is first of all presented; then, with the occasional exception of studies in "love-melancholy," some kind of devastating shock is prepared; finally, as the result of shock working upon the already aggravated humor, the unfortunate character is driven insane. Perhaps the best examples of this comparatively sound theory, which stems directly from the accepted Elizabethan principles of mental disease, are Ophelia, King Lear, Webster's Ferdinand and Cornelia, Massinger's Sforza, and Ford's Meleander, Penthea, Bassanes, and Giovanni. In each case a tendency toward melancholic depression, toward dotage resulting from love-melancholy, or toward jealousy is established early in the play; later, a shock is delivered and results in the apparent adustion of the humor and consequent insanity. With the exception of Shakespeare's Lady Constance, who is a comparatively incidental study of choler encroaching upon dotage, there is only one fairly convincing Elizabethan dramatic study in madness before 1601; that, of course, is Hieronimo. But in his case, as is certainly true of Titus Andronicus and Greene's Orlando, the shock appears to have been delivered before any obvious tendency toward a humor is suggested. The English playwright, before the year 1601, appears, consequently, to have been influenced primarily by Senecan dramatic interpretations of madness and only incidentally by the newly established Elizabethan theory of humors. In the brief and inadequately motivated insanities of Titus Andronicus, who fires arrows at the gods, and of Orlando, who likens himself to Hercules, there are definite suggestions of the influence of Seneca's *Hercules Furens,* in which, first of all, insanity is inflicted suddenly and without pathological cause upon the hero, who then, strongly suggesting the further influence upon Andronicus, draws his massive bow and, firing off stage, unwittingly slays his wife and children. Consequently, although in symptoms and in circumstances Kyd's Hieronimo, as well as his lost Hamlet, undoubtedly had some influence, for example, upon Shakespeare's Hamlet, there appears to have been a sharp change in the dramatic interpretation of madness after 1600. Insanity was no longer, as a rule, motivated, according to Senecan principle, by shock only; a little belatedly perhaps, the theories of Bright, and especially the pathological necessity for an initial humor tendency, had acquired a firm foothold upon the English stage.

Although the playwright, in creating his mad characters, often had more eminent purposes in mind, such as plot motivation and occasionally a desire to symbolize the futility of human effort, nevertheless it was to the established pathological theory of the times that the insane study primarily owed both its form and the method of its treatment. Even Shakespeare, despite his great interpretative genius, appears markedly indebted to the current Elizabethan psychology; the undertones were Shakespeare's, but the broad outlines of his pathological studies, in contrast to those that had conformed with Senecan principles, were obviously influenced by the Elizabethan theories of mental disease. Several times Shakespeare makes a direct acknowledgment to contemporary psychology as, for example, when Hamlet observes:

But I am pigeon-liver'd and lack gall
To make oppression bitter.[11]

In other words, Hamlet, aware of his own shortcomings, is saying that gall is the necessary substance of temper. Shakespeare, indeed, like his fellow dramatists, repeatedly refers to "melancholy," "gall," "liver," and occasionally to "spleen," in their pathological interpretations; I have noted, however, that both Shakespeare and, particularly, Tourneur are more inclined to use the word "spleen" to indicate, in its popular but not pathological interpretation, the seat of anger. In such a case, popular tradition, reduced to slang expressions, certainly is to be preferred in dramatic dialogue to a pathological correctness. The main points are, first, that Shakespeare and his fellow dramatists, notably Webster, were in their many allusions not only consciously but also accurately aware of the prevalent psychiatric theories of their time and, second, that their psychopathic studies, beginning about 1601, probably with Shakespeare's *Hamlet,* indicate not only a sharp departure from any marked suggestion of Senecan influence, but, still more significantly, a reasonably careful adherence to the humor principles of Bright, in particular to the basic requirement of an innate humor.

Juan Huarte, the Spanish physician, also expounded a humor theory and, like Bright, he furthermore was directly indebted to Galen. Huarte's work, *The Examination of the Various Aptitudes for Knowledges,* first published in 1580, and known, probably through the French, through the Italian, or through a private translation, in England well before 1600,[12] was, as the title indicates, much more concerned with the peculiarities of behavior and with occupational fitness than with an exhaustive study of mental disease. In explaining his theory of behavior, Huarte, however, although with somewhat less thoroughness than Bright, necessarily speculated at some length upon the pathology of humors. But only rarely, and then, for example, when he was discussing the abnormal predominance of heat, one of his four "first qualities," did Huarte venture into an interpretation of the causes of actual insanity.[13] Bright's objective was to expound melancholy as a mental disease; Huarte's purpose, more universal in its aims, was to explain the temperament of man and the everyday eccentricities of human behavior. The basic "first qualities," according to Huarte, were the hot, the cold, the dry, and the humid. He explained that one or more of these "first qualities," which by their particular combinations constituted the "temperaments," predominated in the human body at the expense or exclusion of the others. He considered perfect equilibrium impossible; consequently, every individual had his own predominant "quality" or humor resulting in eccentricities that made him in some form or another a misfit in society. Shakespeare, for example, in sympathy for the personal integrity and self-possession of Brutus, was mindful of the social, in contrast to the strictly medical, theory of humors when he wrote:

His life was gentle, and the elements
So mixed in him that Nature might stand up
And say to all the world "This was a man!"[14]

Brutus was almost, but, as circumstances had already proved, not quite the perfect man. According to Huarte, the perfect man, adaptable to all situations, had never or could never exist; near perfection, an approximately close balance of the "first qualities," was the best a man could hope for. For the most part, however, men were eccentrics in varying degree, unfit, unadapted, except for one specific calling in life.

Huarte, furthermore, having consolidated the teachings of Galen, whose psychological theories had often been more general than specific, repeatedly stated in his book that three of the "first qualities"—the dry, the hot, the humid—acted, *respectively,* upon the intelligence, the imagination, and the memory. Consequently, according to Huarte, one part of the brain by the predominance of a particular "first quality" was developed at the expense of the others, and, if excessively developed, led not merely to a particular aptitude, but also to a pronounced eccentricity of character. As Bright, like Galen, made no clear-cut distinction between the parts of the brain that might be affected by a particular humor, it is interesting to compare Kitely's well-known speech on jealousy in Jonson's *Every Man In His Humour* with the foregoing theory of Huarte:

For, like a pestilence, it [jealousy] doth infect
The houses of the braine. First it begins
Solely to work upon the phantasie,
Filling her seat with such pestiferous aire,
As soon corrupts the judgement; and from thence,
Sends like contagion to the memorie:

. . . .

Till not a thought or motion in the mind
Be free from the black poison of suspect.

Consistent with what Huarte had written, Jonson has said in effect
that the heat of jealousy first acts upon the imagination, and then
by surcharge indirectly corrupts the other two "houses" of the brain;
in other words, the excess of a particular humor or "first quality"
has infinitely augmented the faculty of one part of the brain, but
has destroyed the natural aptitudes of the other two parts.

Partially in consequence of this similitude, but also for a much
more fundamental reason, the Jonsonian theory of humors indicates
a much closer debt to Huarte's theory of behavior than it does to
Bright's treatise upon mental disease. Jonson was not interested, as
a rule, in depicting cases of actual insanity; he was instead interested
in the everyday man of the streets and what was wrong with him.
Therefore, the Jonsonian theory of humors, since it was scientifically
concerned not with mental disease and insanity, but rather with the
peculiarities of temperament that resulted from a predominant
"quality," was consistent with the almost certain influence of Huarte.
When, in the well-known induction to *Every Man Out Of His
Humour,* Jonson attacked the misrepresentation of mere whims,
such as affectations of dress and speech, as humors, he was very
clearly correcting and reëstablishing the humor doctrine of temperament and behavior rather than stating a theory of actual mental
disease. There were, consequently, two separate doctrines of humors,
one a medical theory, the other a social theory; both, however, had
their roots in the basic elements of the four humors. Finally, their
distinction as they were defined in the treatises of Bright and Huarte,
respectively, was primarily, although not entirely, one of degree
rather than of kind. The medical or pathological theory became the
basis for the interpretation of insane persons in tragedy; the theory
of temperament, as Jonson was quick to realize, was much better
suited to comic characterization.

There was, therefore, in addition both to the popularity of Bethlehem Hospital and to the contemporary theories of mental disease as partially set forth by Bright, a third and equally specific influence that helped to formulate the abnormal dramatic characterizations of the Jacobean period. Indeed, a few of the eccentrics that evolved from the Jonsonian theory of humors had a more emphatic touch of bedlam about them than did many madmen evolving from the strictly medical theory. If characters like Morose, Zeal-of-the-Land, and Middleton's Follywit lacked the distinction of being completely insane, they made up for it by putting their wits, such as remained, to the contrivance of incidents that were marked by such stupendous abnormality as to be beyond the much less rational capacity of an actual madman. Therefore, if the Jonsonian theory of humors did not, except in such extravagant cases as Trouble-All and the Passionate Lord, result in presentations of actual insanity upon the stage, it nevertheless made a marked contribution to the temper of abnormality that was both to disfigure and to invigorate a major part of the Jacobean drama.

II

It is well to consider briefly the background against which the Jacobean playwright portrayed his mad folk. In a world of sunlight or against a pastoral backdrop of June flowers, a madman as a serious study would be very much out of place. But there is little sunlight in Jacobean drama, and almost none at all in its tragedy. Quite on the contrary, many an intellectual Jacobean,[15] whether disturbed by England's political and social unrest or by the breakdown of the Ptolemaic theory, was a recurrent interpreter of the causes that seemed to have determined the instability of human society. To the tragic playwright, and particularly to Tourneur and Webster, the human being, in sharp contrast to the Marlovian superman, had become little more than a cog, an ineffectual puppet, in a universe that often and intangibly destroyed him; for example, as Webster's Bosola observes, "We are merely the stars' tennis-balls struck ... which way please them." Moreover, as man was no longer the unchallenged principal element of the now poorly understood universe that surrounded him, the playwright appears to have been convinced that he had also become morally irresponsible. Deprived of much of his medieval and Elizabethan significance, man, according to the Jacobean tragic playwright, found his chief and sometimes only justification in preying upon and destroying his fellow men. Consequently, most Jacobean tragedies before the time of Ford not only emphasize the idea of the inconsequentiality of man, but are also staged against a social background of Machiavellian intrigue. Upon this background the mad folk and distraught characters are depicted; some are driven to madness, because, like Macbeth or Fletcher's Maximus, they are fundamentally good men who have acquired a demoralizing passion for evil; others suffer insanity, because, like Webster's Cornelia, they cannot compromise their moral viewpoint with the code of a society in which success is dependent upon evil and deception.

Machiavelli, in *Il Principe*, of which there was at least one good English translation before 1600,[16] had taught the Jacobean playwright two things: a method, not altogether new, by which a man could get ahead in a world where everybody else, figuratively or actually, was trying to cut his throat; and the hypothesis that man was innately evil. In the first instance, the idea was to surmount malice with malice, craft with craft; such a policy was justified only by the second hypothesis, because, if the majority of people in politically responsible positions were good, the need for malice or craft would not exist. There are, moreover, several allusions in Jacobean drama that directly attest to the widespread influence of Machiavelli's theories in England. In Chettle's *The Tragedy of Hoffman* (1603), for example, the blockhead prince Jerome, who has been disinherited by his father from the dukedom, resolves to get even and threatens: "I'll seek out my notes of Machiavell." His accomplice Stilt instantly observes: "Ay, faith, he [Machiavelli] is so odd, that he hath driven honesty from all men's hearts."[17] These quotations suggest two important things: first, that Machiavelli's book was sufficiently esteemed to warrant the reader's making notes of it; and, second, that many an Englishman upon reading Machiavelli had observed the advisability of the practice of a calculating wisdom, together with its attributes of malice and craft, at the exclusion of honesty. By 1603, consequently, an up-to-date moral perspective that clearly comprehended the underlying malice that attends worldly success was quite definitely active in the literary circles of London; and, as the repeated Machiavellian scenes of Jacobean tragedy clearly indicate, the playwright, as a student and inquirer of human motives, was apparently one of the most impressionable interpreters of *Il Principe*.

If Machiavelli, together with the Italian melodrama of Cinthio and his followers, was an almost certain influence upon the settings of political intrigue that were used as background in many Jacobean tragedies, these backgrounds of political intrigue, in turn, influenced the conception of a distinct type of malcontent—the pseudo-madman. Although not actually mad, such malcontents as Malevole, Hamlet, and Flamineo employed the symptoms of madness both to disguise their own intentions and to foil the intrigues of their political opponents; in so far as they sought to foil craft with craft, they were themselves a part of the Machiavellian machinery of the play. Consequently, among the mad folk that we shall find portrayed in the next chapter as part of a society devoted to intrigue and politically motivated wickedness, not the least conspicuous will be the malcontents who feign madness and who, like the Bedlamites, are primarily a Jacobean product. But they are peculiar to the Jacobean stage for a quite different reason: the writers of no other period in English drama seem to have been as poignantly aware of the evil that may from time to time exist within the human society. The Jacobean malcontent not only reflected upon this evil, but also, although not necessarily wicked himself, was forced by the moral decadence of his environment to disguise himself as the madman or the fool; he was part of a world in which ape and tiger stalked each other, and, being at a disadvantage, he wisely resorted to the superior cunning and dissimulation of the ape.

4

Whereas the obvious and basic purpose behind the use of Bedlam-ites by the playwright was to provide spectacular entertainment, the Jacobean pathological studies of mad folk had not one but several fundamental objectives. In the first place, these interpretations were, as a general rule, essentially functional to the plot, as with Macbeth, Lear, and Ferdinand. Secondly, like the Bedlamites, they almost invariably served the playwright as mediums of spectacle. Finally—and certainly most significant—many of them, such as Hamlet and Cornelia, were quite apparently intended as the symbolic expressions of human disillusionment; as such they both illustrate and reflect the evident skepticism that marked the intellectual thought of the period. Just to what extent the incertitude that had resulted in part from the disavowal of the medieval concept of world order[1] actually influenced the pathological studies of the Jacobean playwrights is difficult to estimate, but the mad folk themselves, notably Lear, Timon, Cornelia, and the pseudo-madmen, are made to comment repeatedly on the instability of man's society; furthermore, both the frequent use of distraught and insane characters personifying the idea of human inconsequentiality and the dramatic stature that they often attained clearly attest to the supposition that they were pecu-liarly representative of the Jacobean frame of mind. In short, then, pathological studies of mad folk were an unusually fortunate medium to the playwright; not only did they both readily motivate his plot and provide spectacular entertainment for the audience, but they also offered him an opportunity to express in unusually artistic terms his misgivings about the world in which he lived.

I

Regardless of the playwright's immediate and more fundamental objective, the actual delineation of most of his psychopathic characters was dependent upon contemporary psychology, several tenets of which have been discussed in the preceding chapter. I pointed out, for example, the major difference between Elizabethan dramatic studies of madness, such as Titus Andronicus and Greene's Orlando, and those of the Jacobeans and showed that, in the case of the latter, not only shock but also an initially conceived humor was an essential factor of the study. In many lesser ways the mad folk of the Jacobean playwrights repeatedly give evidence of their conformity to contemporary theory, but it is better to consider these more individualized similarities as we review the insane studies, one by one. As a precaution, however, we should take into consideration Mrs. Forest's article entitled "A Caveat for Critics Against Invoking Elizabethan Psychology."[2] In it she objects to the interpreting of any Elizabethan or Jacobean dramatic character by contemporary psychological theories. Read Burton, Mrs. Forest advises; then try to explain Hamlet or any of the other mad folk by the conflicting theories of humors that seem to have prevailed in Jacobean times. According to Mrs. Forest, every playwright was his own theorist. Her argument against explaining Elizabethan and Jacobean characters by what she considers the conflicting humor theories of the time is certainly not ungrounded, even though she has overlooked a number of specific examples of indebtedness. Burton, as she points out, is evidence of the multiplicity of beliefs. Some consideration, however, must be given to the fact that this ironically genial Oxonian could never turn down a good quotation and that many of the opinions which he quoted had, in his own day, been long since antiquated. For example, when he looks back with perplexity over a long subsection in which he has cited innumerable and contradictory opinions upon the symptoms of melancholy, Burton writes, almost in despair: "The tower of Babel never yielded such confusion of tongues, as the chaos of melancholy doth variety of symptoms."[3] In the next subsection, however, relying directly upon Elizabethan psychology, he plants his feet on more familiar ground, and offers his own interpretations of the symptoms of melancholy, most of which are consistent with both Bright's opinions and contemporary belief. He still speaks of the infinite symptoms arising from humors, but restricts them to broad, but fairly definite, patterns of cause and effect. He observes, for example, of the humors that all depends on "whether they be hot or cold, natural or unnatural, innate or adventitious, intended or remitted, simple or mixed"; he speaks, further, of "their diverse mixtures and several adustions." In a word, Burton, however perplexed he may appear to be by the variety of symptoms, definitely recognized that there are certain basic and established laws, which in the main determine the behavior of melancholic persons. In discussing these laws, Burton is entirely dependent upon contemporary psychological theory. He recognizes, for example, that natural melancholy is cold and dry, that it produces sluggishness, dullness, and solitariness. He argues that unnatural melancholy, which is the adustion of any humor, creates violent emotions. On this point he quotes Bright, noting especially the "excessive distemper of heat turned . . . into a sharp lye by force of adustion." Choler, says Burton, "so adust and hot, degenerates into madness"; adustion of melancholy, on the other hand, leads its victims to being haunted by "black men," devils, chimeras. Sometimes the victims imagine "they are beasts, wolves, hogs . . . bray like asses." All this, despite Burtonian exaggeration, accords with the hideous fantasies mentioned by Bright. It is difficult for me to agree with Mrs. Forest that the Jacobeans did not recognize fairly well-established psychiatric theories and that the playwrights were not indebted, at least in large measure, to contemporary psychology.

II

One of the most memorable of Jacobean dramatic interpretations, a study not unworthy of Shakespeare, is Webster's delineation of Duke Ferdinand in *The Duchess of Malfi*. As a pathological study, he is a fair example of Webster's technical inconsistency; but we shall also find that at the core of this interpretation is an understanding of Elizabethan psychology. Furthermore, in one instance, in an instinctive comprehension of the underlying causes of sadism, Webster, like Shakespeare, anticipates the psychological theories of modern times.

The study of Ferdinand appears to be inconsistent primarily because there is no obvious external cause for his obstinate determination that his widowed sister, the duchess, shall never marry again. But this inconsistency actually adds to the plausibility of the study. In the practice of psychology, for example, how often is it possible to determine readily the *exact* cause of an obsession? Indeed, the problem of discovering the root of Ferdinand's insanity provokes the reader's curiosity throughout the play and, if we are bewildered, we are none the less convinced of the authenticity of Webster's presentation of madness. We can be reasonably sure only of the fact that Ferdinand has repressed a socially abnormal and frustrated emotional urge and that this is responsible, first of all, for his outbursts of anger, later for his sadistic treatment of the duchess, and finally for his madness.

If, however, we consider the pathology of Ferdinand's case apart from the external origins of his obsession, even the incipient symptoms of his madness appear to conform broadly to Elizabethan psychology. The duke, now brooding and jealous, now irascibly explosive, obviously suffers from the compound of two principal humors, melancholy and choler, long before he is actually mad. In each case, furthermore, a pronounced shock is necessary to incite the particular humor to an uncontrollable passion. For example, no more effective shock than the news reporting the birth of the duchess's first child could have been delivered to Ferdinand's choleric humor; it transports him into such "violent whirlwinds" that the Cardinal, his brother, must repeatedly reprimand him. Moreover, as the choleric and now impassioned duke rants, he also betrays for the first time his sadistic impulses:

> Rhubarb, oh, for rhubarb
> To purge this choler![4] here's the cursed day
> To prompt my memory, and here 't shall stick
> Till of her bleeding heart I make a sponge
> To wipe it out.[5]

He, furthermore, threatens, among other heated irrationalisms, to "boil their bastard to a cullisse."

Webster fortunately realized, as few other Jacobean playwrights did, that even the most uncontrollable passions must subside. During his next two appearances, Ferdinand, intent only upon discovering his sister's paramour, is depicted as comparatively collected and calm. If in the first of these two scenes we sense emotional exhaustion, in the second one we begin to feel a conscious effort at restraint; beneath a calm exterior Ferdinand's exhaustion is wearing off, and his emotions and anger are again gathering to a head. Moreover, the restraint that he imposes is not that of the diplomatic intellect, but rather it is the restraint of the melancholic mind that dares not divulge its socially unconformable secrets. He never clearly states his objections to his sister's marriage, but in emotionally taut language warns:

> And for thee, vild woman,
> If thou do wish thy lecher may grow old
> In thy embracements . . .

. . . .

... Let not the sun
Shine on him, till he's dead: let dogs and monkeys
Only converse with him.[6]

So far Ferdinand has shown only the impending signs of madness. His insanity does not actually begin until the melancholic humor has received a highly sufficient shock: the distraught duke finds his sister murdered. The ensuing struggle between sanity and insanity, though brief, is one of the most memorable things in drama. Ferdinand vaguely realizes that it was he himself who ordered his sister's murder, although, as he is careful to recall, "when I was distracted of my wits." A few moments later he inconsistently disavows "this murder"; he imagines that the duchess's death sentence could only have been "registered in hell." His mind strays further:

Oh, I'll tell thee
The wolf shall find her grave, and scrape it up.[7]

He convincingly pulls his reason together long enough to discharge Bosola from his service; then lapses again, this time irrevocably, into insanity.

I'll go hunt the badger by owl-light:
'Tis a deed of darkness.

With this he exits, and is never again as convincing a study. The suggestions of his own imagination have taken root; he actually thinks that he is a wolf, as we are informed by the doctor a little later:

Two nights since
One met the duke, 'bout midnight in a lane
Behind St. Mark's church, with the leg of a man
Upon his shoulder; and he howled fearfully.[8]

The idea that a man could transform himself into a wolf was as ancient as the Greeks; such a metamorphosis was known as lycanthropia, and, as a psychopathic misconception of the diseased brain, it was apparently a recognized theory in Jacobean times. We meet it again in Burton and also in Ford. The delusion, according both to the doctor in *The Duchess of Malfi* and to Burton, was an extreme result of the adustion of melancholy, and Webster, with a ready eye for melodramatic incident, certainly was not unaware of its theatrical value.

As an outright madman, Ferdinand is only once again of functional importance to the plot and becomes primarily a medium of theatricality. First he plays the wolf; a little later, he chases and "throttles" his own shadow; then he shifts momentarily to the practice of patience, and two minutes later, without reasonable provocation, assaults the doctor, who is trying to effect his cure. His behavior is incredible, and yet, as Webster has strongly sketched his character, one already given to extremes even before he is mad, a melancholy and choleric man, disquieted inwardly, feigning patience one moment, raging outwardly the next, this much while still sane, we must admit that in his madness Ferdinand does not far exceed the eccentricity of his earlier conduct. We expect unpredictable behavior, unpredictable symptoms; Webster does not disappoint us, but in depicting the adustion of melancholy he has exaggerated the mad behavior to a point where it becomes incredible to the student of modern psychiatry. Burton, however, in interpreting Elizabethan psychological ideas, was shortly to write that the victims of the adustion of melancholy sometimes "howl like a wolf," some even imagining that "they are . . . wolves";[9] that melancholics are "most violent in all their imaginations";[10] and that "many of them are desperate harebrains, rash, careless, fit to be assassins."[11] Webster, in depicting the later stages of Ferdinand's madness, appears to have gathered together several contemporary concepts of symptomatic behavior and, for theatrical reasons, to have compounded them into a single study.

E. A. Peers, in his book on Elizabethan madmen, suggested that Ferdinand, immediately before he dies, is shocked back into a semblance of sanity. Bosola, for example, comments that the dying Ferdinand "seems to come to himself." Ferdinand, however, has just called the world "a dog-kennel," and this impromptu piece of wisdom happens to be just what the malcontent Bosola thinks of the world. The truth seems to be that the highly imaginative Ferdinand, who a little earlier, in the heat of indiscriminate slaughter, had called for "a fresh horse," prepares to die under the illusion that he is a horse. The speech in which Bosola appears to mark a note of sanity reads:

Give me some wet hay, I am broken winded.
I do account this world but a dog-kennel:
I will vault credit, and affect high pleasures
Beyond death.[12]

The reader's attention is especially directed to the verb *vault*, a word probably prompted by Ferdinand's delusion that he is a horse. Nor can too much, if any, credence be given to the suggestion of sanity in Ferdinand's next and final speech:

My sister, O my sister! There's the cause on 't.
Whether we fall by ambition, blood, or lust,
Like diamonds, we are cut by our own dust.

This observation is not convincing evidence of sanity. It suggests too bluntly that Webster, finally having resolved to give the audience a glimpse of the enigmatic Ferdinand's obsession, is himself speaking through the lips of the dying man.

Although functionally less important to the plot than Ferdinand, Cornelia in Webster's *The White Devil* is somewhat more convincing as a delineation of the causes and symptoms of melancholy as they were interpreted by Elizabethan psychology. Her portrayal is more authentic than that of Ferdinand largely because her madness, in sharp contrast to the spectacular and energetic tempo of the play, is depicted with hardly an iota of melodrama. On the other hand, her only importance to the plot seems to be that her phlegmatic personality contrasts and throws into bold relief the violence that characterizes this play from beginning to end. Furthermore, from an ethical viewpoint, she symbolizes the slender forces of goodness and their inevitable destruction in a world that is predominantly Machiavellian.

Cornelia arrives early and departs late; in the intervening acts of the play we see little or nothing of her. From the beginning she is a mother upon whom the responsibility of children weighs heavily. When she overhears her daughter Vittoria's treacherous confession of illicit love to Brachiano, a confession which is conveyed in the blunt suggestion that each do away with his respective spouse, we can readily appreciate the mother's anguish. She is helpless before the haughty arrogance of her daughter; and when Flamineo, one of Cornelia's two sons, boasts of his unscrupulous methods to obtain preferment at court, which include acting as pander for his sister, the distracted mother, unable to comprehend or cope with such monstrous immorality, cries out: "O, that I ne'er had borne thee."[13]

Cornelia epitomizes virtue, and Webster by depicting her breakdown and subsequent madness shows the incongruity of moral rectitude in a Machiavellian world of evil. Indeed, Cornelia's utter helplessness barely escapes our contempt. When Flamineo dashes on the stage and treacherously murders her other son, Marcello, Cornelia is unable to intervene. A moment later, kneeling by the body, she exclaims: "Let me but give him one heartie kiss, and you shall put us both into one coffin."[14] It is here that we first definitely sense the incipient symptoms of her insanity; we feel her distracting grief, but we are even more aware of the overpowering sense of frustration. Her subsequent dementia is not entirely the direct result of Marcello's death; it results equally from the fact that she sees in his death the utter hopelessness of struggling against the forces of evil. Before she goes completely mad, moreover, her transition from sanity to insanity follows momentarily the fluctuating pattern that Webster, as in his treatment of Ferdinand, handled so skillfully in these climactic moments. When Flamineo confesses his guilt to Brachiano, the distraught mother cries, "Hee lies, hee lies, he did not kill him"; then, breaking loose, she makes at Flamineo with a knife, but at the last instant lets it fall and exclaims: "The God of heaven forgive thee!" At this moment she is an utterly frustrated and completely impotent woman; when we next see her she is definitely insane.

The spectator is informed that Cornelia has "growne a very old woman in two howers" with the "winding of Marcello's coarse." The inner curtain is drawn and the distraught Cornelia is discovered at her work:

> Reach the bayes,
> I'll tie a garland heare about his head:
> 'Twill keep my boy from lightning . . .[15]

She fails to recognize her son Flamineo, and ironically mistakes him for the "grave-digger." A moment later she lapses into the plaintively distracted elegy that begins "Call for the robin-redbreast and the wren." She then concludes her crazed lamentations with a fleeting farewell:

> Now the wares are gone, we may shut up shop.
> Blesse you all good people.

Cornelia's delusions, as explained by Elizabethan psychology, are those of a victim of the adustion of melancholy. Her comparatively unaggressive symptoms, furthermore, are the natural outcome of her second humor, phlegm. Morose and at the same time incapable of action, Cornelia, helpless to offset the repeated impacts of misfortune, has lapsed into deeper melancholy until a highly effective shock transforms the humor to madness. Partially because she was depicted without a real trace of melodrama, she remains, moreover, one of the most authentic pathological studies in the Jacobean drama.

Marston and Tourneur, the immediate predecessors of Webster in tragedy, were likewise concerned primarily with the moral evil of man and his society. Neither playwright, however, has left us what can be considered a strictly pathological study of a full-fledged madman. On the other hand, their tragedies, including Marston's tragicomedy *The Malcontent,* are full of distraught and eccentric personalities that have unusually pronounced characteristics. The reason for these definite personal traits is that most of the characters markedly embody the evil of their immediate society or else, like Antonio and his mother Maria in *Antonio's Revenge,* are driven to distracted behavior by the moral wickedness of the environment. In the main, they are an intrinsic part of a black-and-white ethical problem.

If we except Marston's Malevole, the most memorable of these characters is D'Amville in Tourneur's *The Atheist's Tragedy.* Somewhat like the insanity of Ferdinand, his distraction results from his moral depravity. D'Amville, however, is throughout the play primarily an interpretation of an ethical rather than a psychiatric problem. In worshiping Nature's law of animal survival, he has constantly repudiated every code of civilized morality. In the final scene of the play, he drags the bodies of his deceased sons before a judge, raves distractedly for justice, and then is amazed at the fortitude of his own nephew, Charlemont, in the face of death. He wonders in bewilderment: "What thing there is in Nature more exact than in the constitution of myself." Lest an unworthy man put his nephew to death, he demands the executioner's axe:

I'll butcher out the passage of his soul,
That dares attempt to interrupt the blow.

As he swings the axe in order to execute Charlemont, an unseen hand deflects the blow, and he strikes out his own brains. From the viewpoint of Elizabethan psychology alone, D'Amville's temporary madness, if we exclude the shock suffered from his sons' deaths, would probably be difficult to explain. He appears to have suffered from no well-defined humor. On the other hand, his distraction is a fitting climax to the career of a man who has denied both the existence of God and the necessity for a moral creed among men. Although the theatricality of D'Amville's brief madness is basically Jacobean in concept, the motives behind both it and his death are strongly suggestive of Aeschylean tragedy; since he has willfully contravened the laws of the moral universe, he appears to have been judged and punished by its preternatural agents, which, by Tourneur's interpretation, are identified with the apparent immanence of one supreme Being.

III

Contrasting sharply with the foregoing pathological studies of mad folk are those of John Fletcher. First of all, they are not as a rule depicted against a background of Machiavellian evil. Secondly, their troubles are generally as much or more in their hearts than in their minds. Moreover, with the exception of Aspatia, Fletcher did not create a single psychopathic character of any real importance; and her conception was probably equally the work of Beaumont. Fletcher was primarily interested in theatricality and not in the much broader problems of human insignificance and the moral degeneration of society. Consequently, although his mad and distraught characters may at times suggest the futility of human effort, the emphasis of their portrayal is directed primarily toward the entertainment of the Jacobean audience with the result that they are much more representative of the period than enduring as creations of literature.

Aspatia is the lone exception to the preceding conclusion. As a victim of "love-melancholy," which, according to Burton, usually resulted in "dotage," she differs little from several other interpretations by Fletcher, but the sincerity of Aspatia's grief makes her delineation one of the most convincing to be found in Jacobean drama. She is not, however, mad like Ophelia, nor does she wander into the twilight zone occupied by Ford's Penthea before her death. Her melancholy, nevertheless, is not without theatrical effectiveness; it not only deepens the mood of the tragedy, but it also, and somewhat unconvincingly, motivates the final spectacle of the play when, despairing of death from natural causes, Aspatia is compelled to seek a fatal wound from her lover, Amintor.

As a study in melancholy Aspatia is poignantly convincing upon her first entrance. Her silence provokes our curiosity, and she breaks it only to disavow Melantius's ironic salutation, in which he suggests that she bear her bridegroom Amintor a race of soldiers. She replies, "My hard fortunes deserve not scorn, for I was never proud when they were good," and, without further comment, she silently leaves the stage.

In her next appearance Aspatia is less convincing, but only because grief is best expressed in silence. Bound in a "willow-garland," she takes farewell of Amintor, who has rejected her; but, if her grief is no longer silent, the sincerity of it is no less evident:

> Yet I will take
> A parting kiss . . .
> You'll come, my lord, and see the virgins weep
> When I am laid in earth . . .
>
> . . . .
> So with my prayers I leave you, and must try
> Some yet unpractised way to grieve and die.[16]

In the following scene, after she has poured forth her grief over the needlework of Theseus and Ariadne, the colors of which she would have "more dull and pale," she again lapses into silence, like "Sorrow's monument." Her absence, therefore, during the next two and a half acts is in itself convincing; in the background of our imagination Aspatia remains speechlessly grief-stricken, while we, with increasing apprehension, await the news of her death.

Her appearance "in male apparel" in the final scene of the play is, therefore, a shock. We are suddenly compelled to realize that she is made of sterner stuff than either Ophelia or Penthea. Her survival, furthermore, is altogether inconsistent with the established Elizabethan doctrine concerning lovesick maidens as it was interpreted by the dramatists. The majority of such maidens—Marston's Mellida, Fletcher's Juliana in *The Double Marriage,* and Ford's Calantha—either died of a broken heart or, like Ophelia, their total loss of a sense of responsibility led to death from some other cause. Aspatia, on the other hand, is still in full possession of her wits, despite the extremity of her grief. Beaumont and Fletcher appear to have preserved her primarily for the reason that the play still required a spectacular anticlimax. Her duel with Amintor, furthermore, is certainly neither plausible nor dramatic. It is, however, spectacular and, as "some yet unpractised way to die," it is at least an awkwardly justified climax to Aspatia's grief.

If we should examine the accepted concepts of Jacobean psychology, Aspatia's action in seeking her death is at least remotely explained by Burton; speaking of the victims of love-melancholy, he wrote, "It is still well known in every village how many have voluntarily made away [with] themselves."[17] But this theory does not justify the extravagantly theatrical method by which Aspatia seeks her death. Indeed, if we hope to justify this method, we must turn to modern psychology and in particular to Freud, who would probably have termed Aspatia a masochist[18] and who, furthermore, might have justified her impersonation of a man by the hypothesis that, having lost Amintor, she was symbolizing, as neurotic women sometimes do, the sexual libido that had been so cruelly repressed.[19] Beaumont and Fletcher, however, were not acquainted with Freud, nor did they have the insight into human nature that so frequently justifies the explanation of Shakespearean characters by modern psychology. Their intention was undoubtedly to provide the audience with a final spectacle, and as a result the depiction of Aspatia as a lovesick maiden is made considerably less realistic.

In Fletcher's *Two Noble Kinsmen,* a play in which Shakespeare also had a hand, the compromise between psychopathic theory and melodramatic intention is less apparent; but the compromise is still obvious. The truth is that, if the Jailor's Daughter avoids becoming involved in a single highly melodramatic episode, such as Aspatia experienced, she degenerates into something worse—a farcical figure. As a stage device, moreover, she has the advantage of becoming indisputably insane; for nearly four acts she is not only a convincing pathological study, but also a theatrically effective vehicle. Hence, the degeneration of her depiction at the end of the fourth act into farce is all the more regrettable.

In a functional similarity of the treatment of the Jailor's Daughter to that of Ophelia, we sense the influence, if not the workmanship, of Shakespeare. The cause of her melancholic disposition is unrequited love; but she also, like Ophelia, has a phlegmatic humor. Having failed to find Palamon in the wood, then having wandered apathetically without food or water for two days, she begins to show unquestionable signs of madness:

> I am very hungry:
> Would I could find a fine frog! . . .
> . . . then would I make
> A careck of a cockle-shell and sail
> By East and North-east to the king of Pygmies,
> For he tells fortunes rarely.[20]

Her mind has escaped into the comforting haven of delirium with so little resistance from her powers of will that we are only barely aware of her suffering. When she meets with the country morris dancers, Gerrold inquires: "Are you mad, good woman?" The Daughter replies, "I would be sorry else." She appears to recognize, consistently enough with Elizabethan psychological theory and as Meleander in *The Lover's Melancholy* was to do fifteen years later, the total escape that insanity afforded from unbearable anxiety.

The Daughter's indifference to responsibility becomes more and more apparent. We soon learn that, much in the manner of Ophelia, although not quite as carelessly, she has been sitting knee-deep in a lake, garlands wound about "her careless tresses," and is heard singing incoherent snatches of song.[21] A few moments later she enters, still singing and hopelessly "undone" in her love for Palamon. She unreasonably imagines that "All the young maids of our town are in love with him." Her mind, stripped of all rational restraint and guided only by animal instinct, takes a characteristically vulgar turn,

"There is at least two hundred now with child by him.

. . . .

I'll warrant ye, he had not so few last night
As twenty to dispatch . . ."[22]

Such erotic illusions are generally believed to be the most natural expression of a maiden's demented mind, once it is no longer capable of repressing its most secret and elemental desires. This far at least the depiction of the Daughter follows sound pathological theory; in fact, she is a study worthy the pen of Shakespeare; or, if Fletcher's, she is the work of Fletcher, up to this point anyhow, at his best.

On her next appearance she begins to lose a large share of plausibility. For the convenience of the doctor who is studying her case, she is paraded across the stage; among other things, she rambles incoherently of Dido and of maid's livers "crack'd to pieces with love." Her case is diagnosed as "a most thick and profound melancholy," a diagnosis that accords precisely with Bright's theory that melancholy resulted from a "thickness" of the humor. The staged effect of the scene, however, has already weakened the reader's conviction in the authenticity of her behavior. The doctor's conclusion, furthermore, that her cure will in all probability be effected if the Wooer, her former lover, poses as Palamon and makes love to her in the knight's name is theoretically much too stereotyped. Such a suggestion is primarily a melodramatic device to insure a happy ending, and, since the Jailor's Daughter is nearly as incurable as Ophelia, its immediate result is to translate this hitherto tragic study into farce.

The Daughter's final appearance merely emphasizes the farcical denouement to her madness. She is, quite illogically, depicted as being madder than at any previous time in the play. Even melodrama demands a certain amount of constructional consistency, but, in this final appearance, the Daughter's mental condition makes any likelihood of her immediate cure ridiculous. Her demented mind has degenerated into broken talk about her fictitious stallion, which not only can dance the morris, but also can read and write; furthermore, she imagines a love affair between her stallion and the duke's mare. As a madwoman, she is perhaps no less convincing than upon her previous appearance; but, as a madwoman about to be cured by medical art, she asks considerably too much from the reader's credulity.

Alinda, in Fletcher's play *The Pilgrim* (1621), follows a pattern of "love-melancholy" quite similar to that of the Jailor's Daughter; her cure, however, is definitely more plausible, partly because she is not incurably mad, but even more because Fletcher in curing her avoids the use of a melodramatic device. In fact, Alinda makes a more or less normal recovery. However, if Alinda's cure escapes farce, once cured, but still feigning madness, she certainly involves herself in a piece of extravagant melodrama typical only of Fletcher; her own cure may be believable, but her shrewd appeasement and ultimate cure of the hated Roderigo's immoderate lust deserve to rank high among Fletcher's outstanding achievements in melodrama.

Alinda, not unlike the Jailor's Daughter, first loses her lover, Pedro, in the forest. She likewise suffers from hunger, and, furthermore, is aware that her wits are "wavering." Above all else, she seeks her lover, and prays, "Send me but once within his arms." Disguised and also half-insane, she wanders into a city, where she is apprehended and placed in a house "where people of all sorts, that have been visited with lunacies . . . wait their cures." We do not see her again until after the first spectacle of Bedlamites discussed in the second chapter. Then she is led onto the stage in a condition described as being "a little crazed." She recognizes her lover, the pilgrim Pedro, kisses him immodestly, and exclaims, "My head's wild still!" Burton had recently advocated, for example, the off-setting and curing of one passion by a contrary passion, and this was apparently a popular theory of the time. If Alinda's "head is wild," we feel that it is wild with the bliss of momentarily satisfied love. We sense one passion working against and moderating the other. But this theory by itself does not seem to be necessarily plausible. Her cure is made more logical for the reason that her insanity, although her condition has been aggravated by hunger, had stemmed from the marked frustration of a predominant erotic impulse, and this impulse is ultimately satisfied.

IV

Massinger, like all but one of his contemporaries (the exception is Heywood), quite often relied upon psychopathically abnormal characters for the motivation of his plots. A number of Massinger's depictions of insane and distraught persons are, moreover, nearly as plot-ridden as those of Fletcher. The madness of Overreach, as I showed earlier, is somewhat incongruously imposed upon him by the author for the purpose of climaxing the play with a highly spectacular episode. Several other of Massinger's mad and distraught characters, particularly tragic figures such as Malefort and Theophilus, although functional to the plot, are equally stressed as mediums of spectacle and, if soundly delineated for an act or two, eventually disregard the natural laws of cause and effect altogether. But Massinger, however much he may have exaggerated his pathological studies, also revealed a dependence upon contemporary psychological theory that approaches that of Ford. Unfortunately, however, Massinger's insight into human character was even more shallow than the insight of his greater contemporary; the result is that Massinger's psychopathic studies are frequently little more than stereotyped renditions of theory and lack the finer undertones.

Almira, in Massinger's play *The Very Woman* (produced in 1634), is a study of the contemporary doctrine of love-melancholy. Her symptoms, however, are quite different from those of Fletcher's lovesick maidens, and certainly less subtly portrayed. She is, first of all, not phlegmatic like the Jailor's Daughter; indeed, even though the pangs of frustrated love are chiefly responsible for her insanity, her fundamental humor is choler, and the predominance of this humor determines largely the peculiarities of her behavior. When her despised suitor Antonio, in warranted self-defense, seriously wounds the insolent Cardenas, the highly choleric girl stridently clamors for revenge. Frustrated, Almira is later reported to be the victim of extremely passionate symptoms of melancholy, which are characterized by unruly implorations for her lover Cardenas.[23] When she next appears upon the stage, her behavior is somewhat too stereotyped in its accordance with theory. She suffers a delusion, for example, that her beloved Cardenas is dead, "transformed into a star." But in her distraught mind she imagines that Antonio has suffered a much worse fate. Her memory of him provokes once again the choleric humor. She imagines him howling "in hell, on the infernal rack," and cries: "Do your office, Furies. How he roars!"[24]

Massinger's eventual use of the delusional insanity of Almira shows marked dependence upon a theory recorded by Burton—the belief that a counteracting passion, if severe enough, acted as a cure of the individual's original passion or humor.[25] We find this hypothesis dramatically treated in another play of the period, *The Queen,* reputedly written by Ford, in which inherent melancholy is cured by a fit of jealousy. Also, the irascible father Alphonso in *The Pilgrim* is purged of his original choleric disposition by a period of mental distraction. Massinger seems definitely to have had this contemporary theory in mind in his treatment not only of Almira, but also of Cardenas. Upon recovery from their psychiatric distractions—delusional insanity and soul-searing melancholy, respectively—both are somewhat miraculously rid of their previous and unnatural conceits. Almira is cured of her willful prejudice; Cardenas, of his insolence. The girl voluntarily accepts her jilted lover Antonio, as she was at first supposed to do; Cardenas, once cured of his distraction, which has resulted from his humiliation at having attacked Antonio, becomes, in marked contrast to his former self, the paragon of honor and self-continence.

Insane jealousy, treated at some length by Burton, seems to have been one of the most popular pathological concepts with the Jacobean playwrights. It could forcibly motivate the plot; furthermore, even when restrainedly delineated by such playwrights as Shakespeare and Ford, it invariably led to intense and highly theatrical situations. By its very nature it was conducive to spectacular episodes. It raised the blood pressure; fingers and tempers itched, and swords soon rattled in their scabbards. One of the most effective examples of insane jealousy in Jacobean drama is Sforza in Massinger's *The Duke of Milan.* The study is also informative of Massinger's technique; it illustrates his custom of eventually subordinating a well-defined, although somewhat exaggerated, character interpretation to the purpose of spectacle.

If insane jealousy motivates the climactic action of *The Duke of*

Milan, another humor, perhaps best termed lust-melancholy, not only underlies the psychopathic study but also gives to the action its initial impetus. Indeed, the play itself is a panorama of emotional display, but this is tempered somewhat by a close adherence to pathological theory. *The Duke of Milan* was produced in 1623; two years earlier the first edition of Burton's *The Anatomy of Melancholy* had appeared. The psychological tenor of the play—and the duke himself as the motivating agent is the play—echoes a Burtonian note throughout. The truth is that, although both Massinger and Burton were indebted to contemporary theory, Burton probably exerted a direct influence upon Massinger in this particular play. Burton, for example, had written as follows of love-melancholy: "For such men as are thoroughly possessed with this humour, become senseless and mad, for it is insane love as the Poet calls it, beside themselves, and as I have proved, no better than beasts, irrational, stupid, headstrong, void of fear of God or men."[26] Later, he speaks of a jealous outburst followed by repentance and dotage. Sforza, the duke of Milan, is an almost exact embodiment of these principles.

The duke at first is distinguished merely by his abnormal love for his wife Marcelia, whom he constantly dotes upon. His drooling devotion has none of the charm of Orsino's sentimentality in Shakespeare's *Twelfth Night.* Instead, its bestial senselessness tends to repel the reader. When it is necessary for Sforza to make a foreign journey, he orders Francisco, his minion, to murder Marcelia if it is learned that he himself has been put to death. So obsessed is the duke by the single and sordid passion of his love that he cannot bear the thought of anyone else physically enjoying the duchess even after his death. Consequently, after his safe return from abroad, and after he has been convinced, though falsely, that his wife is an adulteress, his once doting lust is transformed into headstrong and irrational jealousy. This was an emotional eruption which, according to Burton, was the natural outcome of immoderate love, once it had been denied its purely self-interested fulfillment. If we are to believe the animal abnormality of Sforza's love for his duchess, we must above all believe the consequences of its frustration. Half-insane and incapable of reasoning, the duke confronts and ruthlessly murders his wife.

So far, despite his abnormality, Sforza has been consistently portrayed. But less, I think, may be said for the dotage that follows his repentance. Here we find the duke mourning over the carefully preserved body of his wife, whom everybody except him knows to be dead. He officiously warns that "the gentlest touch torments her." Up to this point, however, if we do not reject the depiction of Sforza's abnormal love, the play is still not altogether incredible; but Massinger was an unflagging master of melodramatic denouements, and he could not let Sforza subside into an uninteresting dotage. Consequently, by the author's contrivance, Francisco, disguised as a Jewish doctor and reputed to be a learned man who can bring the dead back to life, returns to court. He paints the cheeks, the lips, and the hands of the corpse; and Sforza, almost witless as a result of his dotage, exults in supposing that Marcelia is awakening to life. A few moments later, the gullible duke, having drunk from the poisoned cup, is a victim of Francisco's ruse and, in dying, aptly observes, "My whole life was a frenzy."

However extreme the study of Sforza's lust and insane jealousy may seem to us, it is an outstanding example of Jacobean dramatic technique. First of all, the playwright has selected a major psychiatric premise that, by Jacobean standards, was unusually concordant with theatrical effectiveness. Secondly, where theory failed to maintain the emotional extravagance, he was able to concoct a spectacle that for sheer abnormality of contrivance has few rivals in the drama. Ingenuity of invention, not dramatic plausibility, was Massinger's predominant talent; in this respect he was in as close harmony with the taste of his audience as was the even more theater-wise Fletcher. Indeed, in the sheer art of surprising the emotions, although Fletcher was the more flexible, Massinger was—as in *The Unnatural Combat,* for example—much the more forcible and extravagant in conception.

V

After this long preoccupation with the melodramatic extravagance of Fletcher and Massinger, it is a relief to turn to a play in which a mental abnormality is treated simply and amusingly—*The Witch of Edmonton.* Produced about 1622, this play is based upon a true incident. The story and the characters act in accordance with the beliefs in witchcraft that were widely accepted in the seventeenth century. The authors, moreover, deliberately avoid sensationalism by telling their story in a naïve and matter-of-fact manner. Dekker, as one of the coauthors, would rather play hobbyhorse with the irrepressible Cuddy Banks than bring Frank Thorney or Mother Sawyer to trial. Indeed, the comic is so much a part of the tragic that even death is accepted as a necessary flaw in the more important business of living. The tragic elements receive little or no "build-up." By contrast to its contemporary tragedies, *The Witch of Edmonton* is a philosophy of life and not an extravaganza of spectacular episodes.

Mother Sawyer, the witch, gains so much sympathy in the beginning that we are inclined to accept her later evils without positive resentment. In fact, she is nothing more than a melancholic old woman upon her first appearance, no witch at all. As Scot, however, tells us in *The Discovery of Witchcraft,*[27] such old and lonely women, particularly the lame and blear-eyed, were traditionally believed to be witches and, even though they were not immediately present, any ill-fortune or disease occurring in the neighborhood would customarily be attributed to them; such, of course, is the misfortune of Mother Sawyer. Friendless and abused—heartlessly beaten, for example, by old farmer Banks—she deliberately, even though in part to justify her reputation, invokes the assistance of the devil. We are not surprised, therefore, when he shows up in the form of the black Dog; Burton had already partially confirmed this superstition: "A third [type of melancholic] suspecteth every black dog to be the devil."[28] As further justification, Bright some years earlier had substantiated the theory that Satan forever hankers after melancholic persons. Mother Sawyer, under the circumstances, could hardly escape an eventual league with the devil, and it was quite conventional that the devil should assume the shape of a black dog. Once this partnership is formed, however, we might expect the beginnings of melodrama; but, if anything, there is nothing more than justifiable comic farce. The Dog, for example, tricks the lovelorn Cuddy Banks into a ducking in the pond. Later, worse things happen, but they are mingled with many comic episodes, and none of the incidents, not even the tempestuous insanity of Ann Ratcliffe, exceeds plausibility. Court records, for example, candidly inform us that witches rode through the air upon brooms on moonlit nights; but Mother Sawyer, although she eventually terrorizes the countryside, never leaves the ground. She is a witch, but at all times ready to indulge her peasant sense of humor. Through her art, horses go lame, butter will not churn, and the country wives become unusually unmanageable; old Banks, moreover, cannot resist an impulse to kiss the hind side of his cow.

Perhaps Mother Sawyer's nearest approach to the melodramatic is the mystically terrifying invocation to the Dog with which she opens the fifth act, and her subsequent horror when he appears—no longer black, but white. This, however, is good drama, not melodrama; if we are to accept witchcraft and devil-possession, the significance of the Dog's change of color remains well within the limits of plausibility. The important point is that the melancholic Mother Sawyer, if we do not count Shakespeare's tragedies, is one of the most honestly delineated pathological studies in Jacobean drama. Once she becomes a witch, furthermore, her powers of magic are always confined well within the limits that had been established for her art.

Like the preceding play, the much earlier *Yorkshire Tragedy,* which was produced in 1605, is concerned with the supernatural powers of the devil and is likewise based upon a true episode. It is, however, not a study of witchcraft; instead, it provides substantial evidence that, where natural causes were not apparent, the medieval idea of diabolical possession was still considered a major cause of insanity. The hero-villain, upon coming to his senses after the crazed murder of his two older children, confesses, "Now glides the devil from me, departs at every joint." Since the father is otherwise an apparently healthy man, only the devil, according to the analytical Jacobean mind, could have prompted him first to his extravagant manner of living, and later to the wholesale slaughter of his family. This conception of madness merely illustrates the fact that the theory of devil-possession, apart from witchcraft, lingered long in the superstitious minds of the people; but the type is not widely representative of insanity as portrayed by the worldly-minded Jacobean playwright.

VI

In briefly interpreting the foregoing studies of insane persons, I have noted in each case the specific and individual similarities to contemporary theory. What, then, in addition to an initial humor-tendency, which is common to all but two of these studies of mad folk, are the general resemblances? The answer is simply that there are two or three other broad theories of Elizabethan psychology that are markedly illustrated by different groups of the preceding characters. Bright, for example, had spoken of the mistaken fancies and "tragicall conceits" that resulted from the adustion of melancholy;

this theory is well exemplified by such portrayals as Ferdinand, Cornelia, and the Jailor's Daughter, each of whom at one time or another experiences pronounced delusions. In addition, Ferdinand, Sforza, and Almira, as well as several other notable Jacobean characters, illustrate another basic tenet of Bright, namely, that victims of choler adust are possessed by "rage, revenge, and furie." These basic principles, furthermore, were not only repeatedly employed by Jacobean playwrights, but were also to be elaborated upon by Burton. Consequently, they, and in particular the idea that the adustion of melancholy resulted in pronounced delusions, appear to have been widely considered theories of the time.

The reader has undoubtedly noted that nearly one-half of the preceding studies are concerned with victims of love-melancholy. Burton, of course, was to devote almost one-third of *The Anatomy of Melancholy* to this particular mental affliction. Love-melancholy and its various aspects, therefore, had undoubtedly been a favorite pathological topic with the earlier Jacobeans. Indeed, as the late Elizabethan poet Campion suggests in his lyric beginning "Beauty is but a painted hell," there was theoretically no surer way of going mad than by falling in love:

Sorrow can laugh, and Fury sing:
. . . .
My raving griefs discover
I lived too true a lover;
The first step to madness
Is the excess of sadness.

An experienced psychiatrist could hardly summarize the causes and symptoms of Ophelia's or the Jailor's Daughter's madness more compactly than the unwitting Campion has done in the preceding verses. There is, however, nothing highly unusual about the idea that an unfortunate love affair can lead to psychopathic complications. What is unusual is the fact that the Jacobean psychologists, poets, and playwrights not only gave such constant and pronounced stress to the importance of love-melancholy as a species of insanity, but also, as many of Burton's conclusions about it help to testify, agreed very closely upon the predominant symptoms of this type of madness.

The theatricality of the mad folk discussed in this chapter is, I think, evident. I have not always made their functional value to the plot quite as apparent. It is an obvious tenet, however, that people of abnormal traits motivate unusual and very often important actions. Consequently, for the most part, the Jacobean playwright found in psychiatric studies a very satisfactory motivation not only of detached episodes but also of the plot. Only on a few occasions, particularly when the traits of the mad folk are markedly phlegmatic, as in the study of the Jailor's Daughter, is the psychiatric interpretation more or less separate from the main action. As a rule, the decidedly positive abnormalities of the insane studies, except when they become helplessly lunatic, made them indispensable agents of the boisterous type of plot so dear to the Jacobean audience. In consequence, such mentally active mad folk as Macbeth, Ferdinand, Almira, and Sforza, as well as their innumerable but less distraught brethren, were not only essential to, but are today unusually representative of, the conception and the spirit that underlay the Jacobean drama, and in particular its tragedy. Without them, the Jacobean plot could hardly exist as a distinct type, since its distinction is dependent largely upon its vigor, that is, the urgent tempo of its action, counteraction, and surprise.

VII

Melancholy, by Jacobean interpretation, was not only considered a disease of the mind tending toward insanity; but also, if "mixed with blood and somewhat adust," as Burton tells us, melancholy, although still a disease, might result in the most subtle kind of wit.

Burton, furthermore, quotes Aristotle to the effect that there is "no excellent wit without a mixture of madness."

The best examples in Jacobean drama of melancholy "mixed with blood" are its malcontents. Marston's Malevole and Webster's Flamineo and Bosola, for example, are naturally somewhat sanguine characters. The former two, for political purposes, feign their melancholic humors; Bosola, however, in the manner of Hamlet, superimposes a touch of madness upon the natural melancholy from which, in addition to his sanguine tendency, he already suffers. Along with Tourneur's Vindici and Marston's Antonio, these three men are not only pretenders to madness, but also mediums of wit.

The malcontents of Jacobean drama, furthermore, are invariably the products of a Machiavellian society. Most of them are essentially good men, each of whom is compelled by the moral evil of his environment to assume a disguise of madness in order to camouflage his own political intentions. Even Bosola, despite his political compromises, is innately virtuous. Flamineo alone is evil; but, like the others, he must assume a "bitter melancholy . . . to keepe off idle questions." The advantages of playing the madman for political purposes, moreover, are perhaps best evaluated by Antonio, who observes:

By wisdom's heart, there is no essence mortal
That I can envy but a plump-cheek'd fool:
O, he hath a patent of immunities
Confirmed by custom, seal'd by policy,
As large as spacious thought.
. . . .
He bears an unturned sail with every wind:
Blow east, blow west, he stirs his course alike.[29]

This in Marston's interpretation was the core of the theory. Among the intrigues of a Machiavellian court, a fool or madcap passed unnoticed except as a source of amusement; he could be on any side or all sides at once. Meanwhile, if his madness was merely feigned, he could disclose intrigue upon intrigue, match deceit with deceit, and still turn with every wind. In the end, as the drama of the period testifies, the pretender to madness was usually successful; at the critical moment he would throw off his disguise, strike home his advantage, and, with melodramatic finality, turn the villain's conceit and self-assurance to ruin.

We learn best, if somewhat paradoxically, from Flamineo, who in the end is the least successful of the malcontents, how the part should be acted. Concerned about his complicity in the murder of Camillo, he decides that he had better "Faine a madde humour" and play the "politicke mad-man." He straightway interprets the conduct of the malcontent in terms that fairly accurately state the Jacobean concept: he will, for example, "talk to any man, heare no man"; he will follow a policy of being "unsocially sociable"; he will rail rather than communicate. In brief, the success of the malcontent who feigned his madness depended largely upon his giving the impression that he was mentally incapable of any responsible action that might conflict with the political motives of his associates. His main purpose was to be corrosively amusing.

According to the evidence of Jacobean drama, persons of great estate usually had particular confidence and trust in malcontents. Malevole, Vindici, and Bosola, each in turn, are the confidants of ministers of state, princes, or dukes. The reason for the trust placed in the victims of melancholy when "mixed with blood" is somewhat difficult to understand. It seems to have been based partially upon their wit on the one hand and their lack of responsible judgment on the other. The malcontents of Jacobean drama invariably possessed a calculating wisdom; at the same time, like the fool of the Elizabethan stage, they appeared to their associates to be indecisive in leadership, and incapable of taking any positive action on their own initiative. For these reasons, they were deemed proper and trusted persons who might release their pent-up energies in the service of others; their talented minds merely required proper direction. This, however, can be considered only a partial explanation of the unusual confidence that people of great place often had in the pseudo-madmen of Jacobean drama. Duke Ferdinand, who has taken Bosola into his confidence, suggests, furthermore, the fact that a melancholic wit served as a passkey, so to speak, to the various political factions within the Machiavellian court. He advises:

> Be yourself:
> Keep your old garb of melancholy . . .
> . . . .
> . . . This will gain
> Access to private lodgings . . .
> . . . like a politic dormouse.[30]

The pseudo-madmen are important, not only because they are a distinctive Jacobean product, but even more because they reflect in unusually concise terms the playwright's attitude toward the world in which he lived. Indeed, the fitness of the malcontents to serve as their author's mouthpiece seems to have been the primary incentive to their conception. The comments of Malevole and Flamineo, and particularly those of Bosola, considered together, constitute as complete a digest of the Jacobean attitude toward the moral corruption of court life as any other type of source available to us today. Hamlet had been concerned primarily, but not entirely, with the limitations of human capability. The malcontents of Marston and Webster, on the other hand, were critical mainly of the Machiavellian practice of evil that was essential to worldly success; and, as characters in a play, they could comment on this moral problem with immunity not only for themselves, but also for their creators. "Make me some rich knave," observes Malevole pointedly; "and I'll make myself some great man." Flamineo, as in other respects, is probably the keenest interpreter of the conduct befitting a man who aspires to political eminence:

O the rare tricks of a Machivillian!
He doth not come like a grosse plodding slave
And buffet you to death: no, my quaint knave—
He tickles you to death, makes you die laughing.[31]

Bosola, however, is the most profound observer of the evils underlying worldly success. Furthermore, his profundity is inevitably veiled in corrosively cynical language that has the ironical effect of beguiling his listeners into an attitude of amusement rather than arousing a sense of injury or offense. When, early in the play, he accepts Ferdinand's gold, he comments:

So:
What follows? Never rained such showers as these
Without thunderbolts i' th' tail of them:
        Whose throat must I cut?[32]

Later in the play, when the Cardinal purchases Bosola's service and promises "honors," he makes a similar remark, but again does not arouse a sense of injury in his employer. He philosophically observes, but with characteristic bluntness:

There are many ways that conduct to seeming
Honor, and some of them very dirty ones.[33]

In the meantime Bosola, whose poignant satirical wit is second only to Hamlet's among the malcontents, makes repeated observations upon the moral degeneracy of court life. For example, he instructs the gentleman who wishes to "be taken for an eminent courtier" as follows: "Let me see; your night-cap expresses your ears sufficient largely. I would have you . . . in a set speech at th' end of every sentence, to hum three or four times, or blow your nose till it smart again, to recover your memory . . . If you smile upon a prisoner, hang him; but if you frown upon him, and threaten him, let him be sure to scape the gallows."[34] Bosola, who obviously reflects Webster's vexation at the hypocrisy of men of position, avoids giving offense only because he can disguise his criticisms in the cynical "humour" of his melancholic wit. In this sense he typifies all the malcontents. These pseudo-madmen were conceived largely to serve as their author's mouthpiece; they were, furthermore, theatrically effective primarily because their pungent satire was subject to dual interpretation: the audience understood their meaning, but their fellow actors ironically discredited their comments and thought them the blunt railleries of a demented mind.

A major reason, then, that most of the malcontents are sharply delineated characterizations is obvious: like many of the actual mad folk of the early Jacobean drama, they are closely integrated with the ethical problem of the play. The idea that moral evil was predominant in human society is the central thesis of the tragedies of Marston, Tourneur, and Webster; and this thesis is constantly and sometimes emphatically illustrated by the critical observations of the pseudo-madmen. Perhaps Marston's Antonio most adequately summarizes the skeptic philosophy of both the malcontent and the playwright; speaking of man, he observes:

His mature age grows only mature vice:
.   .   .   .
Still striving to be more than man, he proves
More than a devil.[35]

5

Besides both the mad folk and the pseudo-madmen that I have discussed, there are in Jacobean drama, and particularly in its comedy, a great many abnormal persons who are just sane enough to avoid the likely prospect of a cell in Bethlehem Hospital. In general, these eccentrics, most of them humor characters, are theatrically no less effective than the full-fledged lunatics. The most noticeable difference in concept is that such characters as Zeal-of-the-Land, Morose, Shamont, and Dampit preserve a pattern of sanity throughout their exaggerated behavior; meantime, their deliberate motives lead to situations often more abnormal than do the involuntary impulses of outright insanity. They are, furthermore, each possessed by a peculiar oddity or humor that is, as a rule, more permanent in nature, although less exaggerated pathologically, than the abnormalities of the actual mad folk. The bona fide humor character, in marked contrast to many lunatics, was not, by the best authorities at least, considered curable.

During the 1590's, increasing attention had been given by contemporary writers to the humor theories. Many poets, like Joseph Hall and Rowlands, seem to have mistaken whims, such as the wearing of a colorful feather in one's hat or of a gaudy scarf that uncomfortably strangled the neck, for humors. Such peculiarities were mere affectations imported from the Continent; they were nothing more than fashions practiced or discarded upon the spur of the moment and were certainly not an innate part of man's nature. A citizen, if he had to spend his last penny, might have his ruff from

Italy, his doublet from Spain, his hose from Flanders, and his hat and its feather from France; if he had been abroad at all, he could wear this assorted costume with a certain amount of éclat, and he would probably emphasize his affectation with a French or Italian accent. Such gallantries, however, such extravagant abuses of taste, were not humors in the proper sense of the word; they were merely whims. Humors, as both Barnaby Riche and Jonson inform us, were far more indelibly ingrained in human nature. According to Galen and, more specifically, to Huarte, the "first qualities," as we recall, determined the fundamental eccentricities of character. Jonson in his induction to *Every Man Out Of His Humour*, in which, as elsewhere, he suggests the direct influence of Huarte, established the humor as a definite literary theory consistent, as I have earlier stated, with both Bright's and Huarte's interpretations, but conforming more strictly to the behavior limits of the latter. In a well-known passage, Jonson specifically reaffirms the nature of a humor; he states:

As when some one peculiar quality
Doth so possesse a man, that it doth draw
All his affects, his spirits, and his powers
In their confluctions, all to runne one way,
This may be truly said to be a Humour.

He adds that affectations of dress, etc., are "more than most ridiculous." Riche, writing in prose, particularized: his State-Ape, for example, is a newsmonger who innately finds gossip a better exchange than money; his Counterfeit Soldier, meanwhile, is an interpretation of the classical *miles gloriosus*, an incurable braggart whom Jonson in the character of Bobadilla had already publicly displayed in the Italian version of *Every Man In His Humour*. By the year 1600, therefore, the social or behavior theory of humors, as distinguished from the psychopathic theory, was firmly established in England and more than anything else was to determine characterization in Jacobean comedy. It arrived at a very opportune moment; for nothing, except possibly the explosive antics of mad folk, could have better suited or embodied the abnormal taste for excitement of both stage and audience.

In the comedy *What You Will,* Marston quite informatively observed that vehement humor characters invariably attracted "a full-stufft audience." From this comment we may readily conclude that the theatricality of the abnormal personality, and not primarily the playwright's interest in the Jonsonian humor doctrines, was the impelling reason behind the long continued use of eccentric characters by Jonson's successors in comedy. Whereas Jonson had been interested fundamentally in analyzing human nature, his successors seem to have shifted the emphasis of humor characterization to its theatrical potentialities, with the result that their portrayals of eccentrics often appear to us artificial and, consequently, inadequate. To them the plot had become the most important element; therefore, the humor studies of Chapman, Fletcher, and Massinger not only at times embody mere whims, but also, even when unmistakably the interpretation of a humor, were often depicted as readily curable, especially when the cure added surprise or impact to the story. In this respect, these playwrights much too frequently deëmphasized the permanent nature of the humor to the status of a whim.[1] But to say that the followers of Jonson had no interest whatsoever in the doctrine of the humors would be somewhat of a misleading, if not a contradictory, statement; we may conclude, on the other hand, that their frequent errors in interpreting the Jonsonian theory resulted almost entirely from an overzealous effort to offer to their audiences theatrically effective characters. Jonson studied his humor characters; his successors too frequently manipulated theirs that they might enhance the number of the spectacles and turns of plot that were demanded by the audience.

I

Although Jonson's basic objective was a genuine analysis of human idiosyncrasy, several of his humor studies markedly illustrate the theatricality that was, as a rule, the natural attribute of dramatic characters that were nearly mad. Perhaps the most evident such character, one who, according to contemporary practice, might have deserved a place in Bethlehem Hospital, is that unusually ardent Puritan in *Bartholomew Fair,* Zeal-of-the-Land Busy. He poses as an evangelist who preaches the abstinence of the flesh, and declaims in particular against the sin of gluttony; but, as an adroit master of sophistic logic, he can readily justify his own private indulgence. Once he is comfortably gorged with pork, this hypocritical "elder of the deacons," a man whose melancholy, like that of the pseudo-madmen, is crossed by a strong strain of the sanguine humor, becomes officiously mindful of his sacred mission. He delivers his tirade in behalf of "the afflicted Saints" against the "foule Faire; and fitter may it be called foule, than a Faire." As he is being carted off by the officers of the peace, the gingerbread woman Trashe acutely remarks, "A poxe of his Bedlam purity." Her implication is, of course, that he belongs in Bethlehem Hospital; this, naturally, is two-thirds talk, but there is some historical evidence supporting the authenticity of the suggestion. According to O'Donoghue in his history of Bethlehem Hospital, more than one mad prophet of the early seventeenth century, including Richard Farnham, who believed himself "an anointed witness," was at one time or another a distinguished inmate of the institution. Farnham's confinement, 1637 to 1638, was a little after Jonson's time; so was the longer confinement of Lady Eleanor Douglas, whose former name chanced to be Eleanor Davies, which she anagramed into "Reveal, O Daniel!" She had also written a treatise, *Strange and Wonderful Prophecies,*[2] based upon the book of Daniel and an anagram system that was quite obviously biased by the ardor of her convictions. As O'Donoghue intimates, Farnham and Lady Eleanor were probably not the first mad prophets to have been confined at Bethlehem. Zealous brethren were quite possibly confined to the hospital at the very time that Zeal-of-the-Land was taking and enjoying liberties at the Fair. Therefore, there is a foundation of truth to the gingerbread woman's curse. Zeal-of-the-Land, however, does not reach Bethlehem; instead, he is placed in stocks, where he is left to prophesy "the destruction of Fayres and May-games."

The evangelistic prophet, once released from the stocks, is finally and emphatically proved to be nothing more than a bag of wind. He tries to close down the excessively lewd puppet show. "Downe with Dagon," he cries, "downe with Dagon; 'tis I will no longer endure your prophanations." Despite the eloquence of his rhetoric, the ranting evangelist is conclusively and humiliatingly argued to silence by one of the puppets.

The ardent Zeal-of-the-Land both personifies and, as a butt of ridicule, is made to satirize the fanaticism of the Puritan. Consequently, what Felltham said about Puritans some fourteen years later is worthy of our attention. In his essay entitled "Of Puritans," he wrote: "But when a man . . . shall . . . be a thief to himself of those benefits which God hath allowed him, or out of blind and uncharitable pride, censure and scorn others as reprobates, or out of obstinacy fill the world with brawls . . . I shall think him one of those whose opinions hath fevered his zeal to madness and distraction." Such at least is an authoritative seventeenth-century opinion concerning a type of character quite similar to Zeal-of-the-Land; and it suggests, without confirming, that the latter, being a public spectacle, may well have been considered insane, or close to insane, in particular by those who did not share the moral perspective of the Puritans.

Whereas *Bartholomew Fair* is a pungent satire upon the vices of comparatively low society, *Epicoene, or The Silent Woman,* is even more incisive as a burlesque of middle-class affectations. In the latter comedy, moreover, most of the vices are the result of mere whims; they are not, for the most part, motivated by inherent humors. The one definite exception to this statement is Morose, a humor character and the central figure of the play; his aversion, moreover, to anything above, and even including, a whisper is hardly a vice; it is an obsession, but a perfectly moral and unobtrusive one. If not quite ready for Bedlam, the neurotic Morose escapes a complete breakdown only by carefully keeping out of earshot of anything louder than a pin-drop. His servants are obliged to answer him by signs; when they must speak, even if in a whisper, Morose is immediately driven to temporary frenzy. Meanwhile, through his nephew's intrigue to marry him to Epicoene, society and all its raucous abuses begin to close in upon him. Morose, although beside himself, temporarily acquiesces. But when the "silent woman" starts talking, the old man's adjustment to society is markedly shaken; and, when the wedding guests arrive and are followed by musicians and trumpets, Morose, nearly out of his wits, takes refuge in the garret, where he promptly locks himself in. Moreover, he is not allowed to recover from his idiosyncrasy; for Jonson, in contrast to some of his successors, rarely, if ever, subordinated his studies of human nature to turns of plot. That is why the abnormal distraction of Morose, like the fanaticism of Zeal-of-the-Land, is not only theatrically effective, but, being honestly enlarged upon, appears surprisingly credible even to the modern-day reader.

Before we leave Jonson and his more exaggerated humor characters, a word or two upon the characters of *The Devil Is An Ass* will not be unfitting. In this play Pug, the devil, borrows a cutpurse's body, spends a day in London, cannot compete with current intrigues and vices, and returns, presumably, to stoking furnaces in Hell. Meanwhile, Jonson makes two uses of contemporary theory regarding insanity. Fitz-dottrel, despite Pug's help, has been thoroughly gulled, but is still hopeful of acquiring his "dukedom"; consequently, he is readily persuaded by the scheming Meercraft to pretend that he was drugged by his "wife's conspiracy" into temporary insanity. The object is to prove that Fitz is possessed by the devil; therefore, after rhyming in his "madness," he breaks out into Greek, Spanish, Italian, and French, as proof, according to Jacobean beliefs, that the devil is in him. More convincing perhaps to the modern reader, and certainly more spontaneous, is Pug's little "Tom o' Bedlam" act earlier in the play. In this incident Pug, trying to escape apprehension for the clothes that he had stolen from Ambler (for, unfortunately, the cutpurse's body had been without clothing), pretends to be a Tom o' Bedlam—that is, a temporarily released or former inmate of the hospital—and talks harebrained nonsense to avoid being pinned down to a direct reply.[3] In this, if in little else, Pug is diabolically successful.

In the consistent genuineness with which he portrayed his eccentrics, Middleton ranks second only to Jonson among the comic playwrights of the period. Dampit, the unscrupulous usurer in *A Trick To Catch The Old One,* is a fair example of Middleton's technique and remains perhaps the most profanely alive characterization of the Jacobean drama. Styling himself a "trampler of time," Dampit has, when we first meet him, already busybodied his way into a fortune by capitalizing on the laziness of others and pressing their lawsuits; but drink has brought him to blasphemous ruin. When his officious servant Audrey tries to coax him from his cups, reminding him that it is time for bed, he roars back at her: "Why, thou base drudge of infortunity, thou kitchen-stuff-drab of beggary, roguery, and coxcombry, thou cavernesed quean of . . . bawdreaminy, I'll tell thee what, I will not give you a louse for thy fortunes . . . Why, thou base, impudent quean of foolery, flattery, and coxcombry, are you answered?"[4] Dampit continues, despite Audrey's objections, to rave in this distracted, but robustly convincing manner; nor will he "to bed" until he has had his glass of "fresh beer."

A little later, Dampit's deathbed scene is a masterpiece of coarse realism. He is now raving drunk, without food for days, his memory eclipsed, while he sits propped in bed, drinking sack; he is "bedridden," as we hardly need to be told, "with drinking." A customer arrives to borrow one hundred pounds. To Dampit's retort that he has but two thousand pounds in the house, Audrey cannot withhold a laugh. Dampit explodes: "Out, you gernative quean, the mullipood of villainy, the spinner of concupiscency!" A few moments later, when Audrey coyly reminds him that the vintner will be his heir, Dampit, whose use of English is based primarily upon phonetic effectiveness, erupts with cryptic violence: "Out, you babliaminy, you unfeathered cremitoried quean, you cullisance of scabiosity!" Meanwhile he fawns upon the wealthy Sir Launcelot, then blasphemes him when he thinks that he is out of hearing: "A louse for his love! his father was a combmaker . . . the superlative rascal!" After further outbursts, he falls to sleep in a drunken stupor, in what is perhaps his last sleep on earth.

As a pathological study of an alcoholic, Dampit is one of the most modern examples of theatricalism in Jacobean drama. Most psychotic symptoms are portrayed today as less extravagant than they were on the Jacobean stage, but the symptomatic potentialities of a drunkard—if we recall such movies as *The Lost Weekend*—have not been appreciably curtailed. Furthermore, Dampit reminds us of a significant difference between the realism of Middleton and that of Jonson. The latter's realism is dependent too precisely upon humor theory; his character investigations result primarily in composites of a type and not studies of individuals. Middleton, like Dekker to a less extent, appears to have presented his material exactly as the eye observed it on the streets and in the taverns of London. In the portrayal of eccentrics, Middleton was realistic rather than perspicacious; he did not theorize or delve under the surface of his material, but sketched the surface with extravagant strokes. The result was that theatricality often became a natural component of his individualized depictions of eccentrics. Of this technique Dampit is not only a good illustration, but also the consummate achievement.

We have already given considerable space to Fletcher's mad folk, particularly to those in *The Pilgrim*. Another gentleman in the same play is all but mad himself; his "madness" is basically the result of reversals, but his mental stability is also impaired by an excess of choler, which, seriously tested through misadventures and disillusionments, ultimately, if not quite convincingly, wears itself out. In the beginning, Alphonso keeps a reign of terror in his house, tongue-lashing daughter and servants alike. When he learns that Alinda has eloped in pursuit of the pilgrim Pedro, he delivers as irascible a tirade as is to be found in Jacobean drama:

Saddle my horses, rogues! ye drunken varlets,
Your precious diligence lies in pint-pots,
Your brains in butts! My horses, ye pin-buttocks!

Almost immediately he adds,

I say again, my horses!
Are you so hot? . . .
Must you be Jumping-Joan? I'll wander with you,
I'll jump you, and I'll joggle you!—My horses![5]

When we next meet him, after his unhappy experiences in the forest, his choleric nature is quite subdued by the turn of events:

I have been fooled and jaded, made a dog-bolt!
My daughter's run away; I have been haunted too.
I have lost my horse; I am hungry, and out of my wits also.[6]

Alphonso's present distraction has largely displaced his choleric disposition; but he never gets any more insane than this. The loss of his daughter and his primary objective of regaining her begin to shape his subsequent actions into something resembling a crusade, and the necessity of concentrating upon his mission acts as a cure of his temporary mental derangement. But Fletcher's ultimate depiction of Alphonso as a man completely rid of his choleric humor is less plausible and, notwithstanding its concordance with a Burtonian theory (see p. 101), is primarily motivated by the author's desire to please the contemporary audience with a surprise happy ending. As Huarte and Jonson had recognized, the eccentricities of temperament are indelibly a part of the individual man.

In *The Nice Valour,* besides the "ill-brewed" Passionate Lord, there are two humor characters that, because they are not completely mad, perhaps more fairly illustrate Fletcher's extravagance of character conception.[7] At least Shamont and Lapet are supposedly responsible for their own incredible actions, whereas The Passionate Lord is not; therefore, we may presume that the behavior of each is guided by some kind of rational pattern. Basically their motives, however eccentric, are not illogical; certain people, for a reason, react much in the same manner as either Shamont, on the one hand, or Lapet; the main difference is that Fletcher's characters exceed, indeed much too far exceed, the normal pattern of idiosyncrasy. Shamont is a satire upon the sensitive courtier who is unable to bear any offense against his honor; this incapability, up to a certain point, is not unbelievable. But Shamont's reactions are carried to an extreme that in itself is incredible. Casually switched by his friend the duke, who is merely trying to attract his attention, he cannot endure the dishonor; his shame is irreconcilable, and he retires in permanent self-disgrace to the seclusion of a country cottage. Lapet, on the other hand, is devoid of the slightest sense of shame; he is at various times "twinged," kicked, "thumped," and "bastinadoed," without feeling any offense. He writes a book entitled *The Up-*

rising of the Kick, hoping to save "a hundred gentlemen a-month" from death by duel. Lapet's motto in accepting the kick is "P-A-T-I-E-N-C-E," spelled out, of course, in capital letters. When The Passionate Lord beats him to the ground, he compliantly remarks, "O, sweet sir!" No abuse, however violent, to his person upsets his equilibrium; he is as phlegmatic and servile as Shamont is sensitive. Fletcher (or possibly Beaumont) undoubtedly created him as a foil to the highly sensitive Jacobean courtier who carried his reputation, if not upon the point of his sword, at least upon his cuff. Significantly, perhaps, the abnormal response or lack of response of Lapet's insensitive nature makes him considerably more effective as a theatrical medium than is Shamont; if a playwright is going to overstep realism and create farcical characters, it is better that no doubt be left that farce is his primary intention.

An interesting play, indeed one of the most interesting of the Jacobean period, is Dekker's *If This Be Not A Good Play, The Devil Is In It.* The reader, however, must not take the title too literally; for the devil is in it, and it is still a good play. If Middleton is primarily a realist and Fletcher, despite farcical characterization, basically a romanticist, Dekker is a hybrid of the two; he can be both, quite often at one and the same time. The present play, a piece of bedlam from beginning to end, is a fair example of Dekker's ingenuity at producing realism of character against a background of romanticism. Pluto, disgruntled over the decrease of new arrivals in hell, sends three devils to earth to strike up some future trade. One of them, who is sent to pose as a merchant, learns more evil from his fellow merchants, particularly from Barterville, than he can teach them. The other two are considerably more successful; Ruffman succeeds so well in corrupting the king and the court of Naples that he indirectly starts a civil war that ruins both king and subjects alike. The roguish Shackle-soul, meantime, in sheer ironical deviltry, outdoes them all; his corruption of the Priory, resulting in the growing of a vineyard and a perpetual drunken orgy among the friars, is in its concept one of the most effectively satirical situations in Jacobean comedy.

Much more to our point, however, is the play's afterpiece, which can perhaps be most suitably described as "bedlam in Hades"; in this scene Dekker turns loose a good portion of the devils and distracted souls of hell. The title page of the first quarto of the play, printed in 1612, merited the following inscription: "As it hath been lately acted with great applause by the Queenes Majesties Servants at the Red Bull." Taking into consideration the temper of the Jacobean audience, we may be fairly certain that it was the afterpiece probably more than the play itself that merited this "great applause." Indeed, rarely did the drama of the period, despite Dekker's realistic characterization, reach such a terrifying pitch of melodramatic excitement. Guy Fawkes, the merchant Barterville, and others are pictured in hell, scalding in fire, madly raving for water, and taunted by devils, who provoke them, among other things, with a burning torch and a handful of snakes. Such unmitigated bedlam, punctuated by the howling of distracted persons, could hardly fail to satisfy the indelicate theatrical appetite of the Jacobeans. In a climactic episode, for example, a devil stabs Ravillac, the French assassin who has only recently arrived in hell, and then with a torch burns his hand off. Ravillac understandably shrieks: "Damnation, furies, firebrands!"

But the distraction of the tortured souls does not end here. Dekker, combining realism with an imaginative perspicacity worthy of Marlowe, paints an even more sadistic picture. Pluto is not satisfied with the present torments of his distinguished guests; he orders them to be lashed with whips of poisoned steel, then ducked nine times in "our brimstone lakes." When brought before the three judges for trial, Fawkes is perhaps the most crazed of the sufferers; he cries: "Glorious bonfire, pontificall bonfire! brave heads to contrive this . . . through fire, through flint; ha, ha, ha . . . enemies to massacre, ha, ha, dismal tragicall comedy now." He runs out, raving, "Am I betrayed? give fire now, now, give fire!" Barterville, however, upon hearing of his sentence is hardly to be outdone; he ejaculates: "My chaine, let me hang in my chaines, so it be my Golde chaine; theeves, theeves, theeves!"

In addition to the effective theatricality of the distracted persons, the satirical purpose of Dekker is markedly poignant. Besides his ridicule of certain notorious individuals, he has, through Barterville, attacked the avaricious practice of merchants in general. Indeed, satire was almost invariably an inherent part of the depiction of comic eccentrics. Jonson, as we recall, used Zeal-of-the-Land as the medium through which he satirized the fanatic zeal of the Puritans; and Fletcher, through his ridicule of Shamont, clearly stated his disapproval of the highly sensitive honor of the Jacobean courtier. Where the study had little relation to plot, the satire was, furthermore, as with the Bedlamites (see Chap. 2), more or less essential to artistic justification. Elsewhere, as in the interpretation of Morose, who is centrally involved in the plot, the satirical implications add considerably to the already present merits of the study. Whatever may have been the other objectives of the playwright in the creation of his highly eccentric comic characters, the inherent opportunities for satire that he exploited contributed in no small degree to both the significance and the theatricality of humor interpretation at large. Whereas, through the exposure of human folly, satire instructs us and thus attains significance, it also adds to our entertainment by universalizing, as a rule, the object of our laughter. This principle, first perfected by Plautus, is the immanent characteristic of Jacobean comedy; without it, the merriment would be markedly diminished.

II

Most of the characters that have been treated in this chapter are overaccentuated humor studies. That the majority of them are consistently, although not always plausibly, portrayed results primarily from the fact that the particular playwright adhered to the basic fundamental that a humor was innate and, consequently, permanent. On the other hand, a great many eccentrics of Jacobean comedy, such as Fletcher's Leon and Belleur and Massinger's Luke, are made much less plausible than they might have been for the reason that their humors are artificially imposed or discarded to suit the needs of the plot. This inconsistency of humor portrayal, furthermore, is considerably more pronounced in the tragedy of the period, primarily because the distraught characters of middle and late Jacobean tragedy, by contrast to a number of comic eccentrics, were almost invariably employed as the chief agents of the plot; in consequence, their mental abnormalities were subjected by the playwright to repeated contrivance in order that they might suit or fulfill the technical functions—that is, the turns of plot—required of the story.

Early in the Jacobean period, such tragic playwrights as Marston, Tourneur, and Webster had been fundamentally interested in the moral evil of the human society. Their distraught and insane characters were created to symbolize, or to be driven mad by, the degenerate evil of their environment and, since such characters were both illustrative of and closely integrated with the moral problem, they were almost invariably consistent in portrayal. But, under the influence of Beaumont and Fletcher, the concept of tragic technique was markedly altered; the surprise element became much more important than the analysis of moral evil, and distraught characters, in consequence, although usually evil, were made more and more predominantly the contrived instruments of theatricality. That is why the majority of highly distraught personalities in tragedy, from 1612 to the time of Ford, are so awkwardly depicted that none of them, with the exception of Webster's Ferdinand and possibly of Massinger's Sforza, is worth the space of discussion. Fletcher's Maximus, Rollo, and Ferrand and Massinger's Malefort and Theophilus[8] are quite typical examples of the distraught tragic figure whose only tangible importance to his play was to motivate a plot laden with surprise elements. Each of them, moreover, is a highly effective agent of theatrical horrors. But, being subject to whimsical and externally contrived abnormalities rather than being moved by an unalterable humor, not one of these five typical characters is a credible personality.

It is also worthy of note that the distraught characters who motivate the tragic plots of Fletcher and Massinger, although they approach madness, rarely become full-fledged madmen. In discussing Ferdinand, I mentioned that, once he became completely mad, he ceased to be the prime agent of the plot. The same, of course, is true of King Lear, whose motives move or influence the story only up to the point where he becomes utterly insane. Psychiatric studies, with the exception of those of insane jealousy, were, as a rule, effective agents of the plot only so long as they retained some possession of their wits. Fletcher and Massinger, therefore, since they were much more interested in plot movement than in character delineation, found distraught characters, and not psychiatric studies that led to insanity, by far the better suited to the motivation of their stories. Indeed, by 1614, plausibly delineated mad folk had all but vanished from the stage; they had, little by little, been shoved from the boards by melodramatically conceived automatons of violence; for the latters' minds, though twisted, were not quite insane and, therefore, were much better adapted to the continued contrivance of episodes that were marked by both impetuosity and horror.

In fact, so neglected had become the art of profoundly analyzing the abnormally diseased mind that in the fourteen years between Webster's creation of Ferdinand and Ford's play *The Lover's Melancholy* there are a score and more of distraught perpetrators of violence in Jacobean drama, but there is not a single madman that is a convincing pathological study. Ford, however, in marked contrast to his contemporaries, was to restore to psychiatric studies much of the authenticity and craftsmanship that they had received in the early part of the period. His achievement, in this respect, will be the subject of the next and concluding chapter.

6

Despite the fact that John Ford's major plays belong to the early part of the Caroline period, the author actually began his career as a playwright at least twelve years before the death of King James. Furthermore, not only do we find reactionary elements in Ford's major plays, such as, for example, the repeated condemnation of the moral evil of man, but also he based his dramatic formulas upon the theatrical traditions of the Jacobean stage, and in particular upon the consistent use of highly distraught characters and of spectacle. Ford, therefore, not only is considered a Jacobean, but also represents (as we shall see) the final phase of a movement that had begun thirty years earlier with Shakespeare's *Hamlet* and Marston's *Antonio's Revenge* and *The Malcontent*. In the broadest sense, Ford, by restoring the dramatic emphasis to character, by making the analysis of distraught or abnormal characters almost invariably more important than the presentation of spectacle, closed the circle that brought the contemporary drama, and in particular its tragedy, back to the point from which it had started. Ford's technique, however, was very different from that of Shakespeare and Webster; the latter, and particularly Shakespeare, although conforming to the broad outlines of contemporary psychology, had employed, for the most part, instinctive insight to mold character. Ford was more painstaking; his distraught characters were the product of careful logic based upon a comparatively scientific knowledge of both Elizabethan and Burtonian mental pathology.

Despite a scholarly approach to his subject matter, Ford also revealed a highly professional attitude toward the theater. Because of his scientific and theoretical interpretation of character, Ford was the type of man whom we might expect to remain a closet drama-tist. Indeed, if one were to remove the spectacle from Ford's first well-known play, *The Lover's Melancholy,* nothing but a closet drama would remain; yet this play was apparently very popular at the time of its first production, although, significantly enough, when revived in 1748, it was a failure. Ford, who was painfully academic in his exhaustive and theoretical treatment of character, especially in *The Lover's Melancholy,* was also acutely aware of the particular type of theatrical fare that was demanded by his con-temporary audience. His technique, then, was twofold: he thor-oughly developed his major characters by a logical and often too scientific interpretation of their underlying motives; and he always employed appropriate and sufficient spectacle to make his plays appealing to the early-seventeenth-century audience. This, however, does not fully explain the much greater literary merit of Ford's plays when we compare them, for example, with the spectacle-ridden tragedies of Fletcher that were written after Beaumont's death. Fletcher, as I have already stated, was not interested in the integrity of character development; he was interested primarily in the spec-tacle that evolved out of the abnormalities of character and situation, with the result that his characterizations were contrived and altered to suit the exigencies of plot. Ford, on the other hand, rarely, if ever, allowed spectacle to become the primary end in itself. The theatricalism in Ford's plays is, with the possible exception of the masque in *Love's Sacrifice,* always justified as the logical result of the underlying motives of his characters. As Miss Ellis-Fermor aptly phrases it: Ford's principal objective was "the deep experience of certain emotions and the clear, distinctive analysis of the experi-ence."[1] In Ford's plays the emotions of the principal characters were painstakingly analyzed; indeed, these emotions were dammed up, so to speak, until they could be restrained no longer; then they were either dissipated in a series of minor explosions or else, despite Ford's restraint, broke their bulkheads with volcanic energy. Spectacle, consequently, was almost always psychologically justified; for even though it was offered as a professional compromise to the audience, it resulted naturally from emotions or circumstances that had already been extensively and consistently analyzed.

I

In the interpretation of madness and melancholy, Burton's *The Anatomy of Melancholy* was the chief guide and psychopathic gospel to Ford. But one must not forget that *The Anatomy* can be quoted to nearly as many ends as the Bible. If in his first outstanding play, *Lover's Melancholy*,[2] Ford had not clearly acknowledged his indebtedness to Burton, the latter's influence on the playwright's later works might well be less evident. However, even if Burton had not been an influence, it is difficult to deny Ford's consistent interest in contemporary psychology. Indeed, if we overlook the dramatic elements, three of Ford's plays would very well pass as dissertations upon psychopathic theory; unlike Shakespeare and Webster, his predecessors in psychiatric interpretation, Ford was at times as much the scholar as the playwright, and in *The Lover's Melancholy* the scholar in Ford was paramount. Dramatically, this comparatively early attempt is hardly a good play; academically, it is one of the most informative works of the time upon the subject of melancholy. It is, in a word, some ten to twenty pages of Burton dissected and dramatized.

In no place in literature is Burton's influence more evident and indisputable than in "The Masque of Melancholy," which, although internally and too logically motivated, is the outstanding spectacle of *The Lover's Melancholy*. In this masque, Ford introduces six madmen, every one of them a direct and intentional plagiarism from

Burton, and, therefore, clearly establishes his scholarly interest in contemporary psychopathic theory. The first madman suffers from lycanthropia, or wolf-madness; indeed, he thinks that he is a wolf, and what he has to say is primarily a colloquial transposition of a passage from Burton's *Anatomy*. Burton, for example, had observed of the victims of lycanthropia: "They lie hid most part of the day, and go abroad in the night, barking, howling, at graves and deserts."[3] Ford's madman is made to say: "Bow, bow! wow, wow! the moon's eclipsed; I'll to the churchyard and sup. Since I turned wolf, I bark, and howl and dig up graves: I will never have the sun shine again."[4] Ford's next madman is a victim of hydrophobia. Of hydrophobia, Burton had written: "Commonly, saith Heurnius, they begin to rave, fly water and glasses . . . see strange visions."[5] Consistently with this interpretation, Ford's victim of hydrophobia, in between cursing his wife for a whore, observes: "It shall be treason by statute for any man to name water . . . Break all the looking-glasses; I will not see my horns: my wife cuckolds me."[6] The third madman is a victim of dotage, a philosopher suffering from delirium. Burton had attributed dotage to "a defect of the organs," among other things, "and over-much brain." Ford's philosopher rants: "Philosophers dwell in the moon. Speculations and theories girdle the world about like a wall . . . I am very, very poor, and poverty is the physic of the soul: my opinions are pure and perfect."[7] Obviously this gentleman, in general consistent with Burtonian theory, had either possessed too much brain or overstretched what little he had.

Ford's fourth lunatic is a woman, a victim of "clamorous phrenitis." "Pride is the ground on 't," observes the physician Corax, who acts as a commentator throughout; "it reigns most in woman." Of these symptoms, Burton had written merely that phrenitis (brain fever) is "clamorous," whereas melancholy is silent. More pertinent, however, is Ford's fifth madman, a "Bedlamite," who suffers from hypochondria. Burton had observed that this type of patient is afflicted with a rumbling as if he had "a serpent in his guts" and "from these crudities, windy vapours ascend up to the brain, which trouble the imagination, and cause . . . many terrible conceits and chimeras."[8] Adhering closely to this interpretation, Ford's hypochondriac rants confusedly:

Hark, did ye not hear a rumbling?
The goblins are now a-tumbling:
I'll tear 'em, I'll sear 'em,
I'll roar 'em, I'll gore 'em!
Now, now, now! my brains are a-jumbling—
Bounce! the gun's off.[9]

Corax, accurately mindful of what Burton had said, explains the Bedlamite's symptoms as the result of "a windy flatuous humour." The sixth and last of Ford's lunatics appears to be equally dependent upon its Burtonian original. She is a big-bellied sea nymph, afflicted with the wanton melancholy; she immediately leads the other lunatics into a whirling dance. Corax interprets her symptoms:

This is the Wanton Melancholy. Women
With child, possess'd with this strange fury, often
Have danc'd three days together.[10]

Ford characteristically has not exaggerated; Burton had observed of "wanton melancholy," or St. Vitus's dance, that great-bellied women afflicted with the disease will dance until they drop apparently dead.

The theatricality of the preceding masque is self-evident; madmen cavort with better than customary energy, even though their symptoms are carefully regulated by the playwright. Ford, by introducing this spectacle, has served two principal purposes: theatrical effectiveness and psychopathic interpretation. In its purpose, in its execution, and ultimately in its results, the masque is a stereotyped rendition of Burton. The doctor Corax has arranged the masque deliberately in an effort to learn the cause of Prince Palador's melancholy; he hopes that one of the Burtonian mad folk may strike a sympathetic note and bring a confession from the prince. Obviously, with one possible exception, the madmen that are brought on the stage are hardly relevant in their behavior to the symptoms of the prince, who is a victim of melancholic dotage; but the masque, as Ford intended, makes good spectacle and sharply illustrates a recurrent principle so peculiar to the Jacobean stage, namely, the belief that symptomatic studies of mad folk, no matter how systematically portrayed, were unusually appropriate instruments of theatrical effectiveness.

But "The Masque of Melancholy" may be considered from a still more critical viewpoint. Since it is both directly motivated from within the plot and featured by carefully analyzed symptomatic studies, this early episode of Ford's major plays foreshadows definitely the tendency toward refinement that characterizes his major works as a whole. Ford's mad folk and his scenes of horror were rarely, if ever, permitted to be either improperly motivated interpretations or melodramatic ends in themselves, but were almost always treated as an integrated and scholarly outgrowth of the author's theories of human conduct. Ford himself in an earlier passage[11] of *The Lover's Melancholy,* a passage in which Corax attempts to explain what melancholy is, had directed the reader to Burton's *The Anatomy of Melancholy.* "Vide," says Ford in a footnote, "Democritus Junior," which was Burton's pen name. Ford, subsequently, was to remain throughout his major tragedies intellectually conscious of the scientific theories explaining human abnormality. But life and human conduct, unfortunately, are seldom quite as clearly comprehensible as Ford tried to make them. Unflaggingly analytical, he was not only to bring character development, the forte of Shakespeare and Webster, nearly to a standstill; he also brought the forcible movement of plot that had characterized the plays of Fletcher and Massinger to an end.

There are, however, at least two major psychopathic studies in Ford's tragic dramas that retain much of the vigor that we expect of the human animal. One is Giovanni, particularly after Ford in the fifth act has ceased to analyze his inner struggle. The other, strangely, if we remember that *The Lover's Melancholy* is the most academic of Ford's plays, is the seasoned dotard of that play, Meleander. Indeed, this antique lord is somewhat too paradoxical to fit into any single pathological theory; unlike Prince Palador, the melancholic hero of the play and perhaps the most stereotyped character in Jacobean drama, Meleander is permitted within limits to develop his own idiosyncrasies. The result is that he helps to save an otherwise dull play from unabated boredom. Even so, Ford was unquestionably conscious of theory in creating, if not always in developing, Meleander. "Close-griping grief," primarily for the loss of his daughter, has made him, to use Burton's words, "as averse to company, as Diogenes in a tub." With his remaining daughter and a servant he lives alone, like a grizzled lion at bay, in an apartment of the castle. From the beginning, it is repeatedly suggested that he is mad; for example, "he sleeps like a hare, with his eyes open." However, Corax, the very officious physician, is probably correct; having diagnosed Meleander's disease, he says, " 'tis not a madness, but his sorrows." Indeed, his sorrows are paramount, and sorrow rather than fear is the key symptom of his melancholy. When we first meet him, one thought, the loss of his daughter, obsesses and deranges his mind:

The raven croaked, and hollow shrieks of owls
Sung dirges at her funeral; I laughed
The whiles, for 'twas no boot to weep.[12]

And so he continues. Old age, added to his rooted grief, has already accentuated his dotage and also, consistently enough, removes any serious effort at emotional restraint. In keeping with his senility, other humors are also at work—choler and a touch of the sanguine.

It is this mixture of humors, a mixture which, according to Burton, produces as "many . . . monstrous fictions as wine doth effect," that differentiates Meleander and makes him infinitely more vital than Ford's characteristically stereotyped interpretations. When the privacy of his seclusion is encroached upon, he ignores the kindnesses of his friends and roars back:

But I'll outstare ye all: fools, desperate fools!
You're cheated, grossly cheated; range, range on,
And roll about the world to gather moss,
The moss of honor, gay reports, gay clothes,
Gay wives, huge empty buildings.[13]

If his melancholy humor makes him dote upon the loss of his daughter, his choler almost invariably expends itself upon the hypocrisy of political intent; and, of course, for a reason: the former prince of Cyprus deprived him not only of a daughter, but also of his public honors.

Despite the complex idiosyncrasies of Meleander, only once does his behavior violate Ford's inherent pattern of logic, and then by excess rather than by the playwright's extraneous invention. This extravagance of behavior occurs upon the old man's second appearance. Meleander's choleric humor, unrestrained as a result of his senility, has momentarily been inflamed by a trivial circumstance to the point of adustion, with the result that his actions border upon the farcical. Brandishing his poleax, he cries:

Show me the dog whose triple-throated noise
Hath roused a lion from his uncouth den
To tear the cur to pieces.[14]

A moment later, the physician Corax, having donned a fierce mask, and threatening to turn Meleander into the "stone, which Sisyphus rolls," effectively thwarts the latter's choleric outburst. The fierceness of the mask is perhaps an unintended stimulus to the old lord's underlying sanguine humor; for, in an effort to pacify his adversary, Meleander retorts:

Hold, hold, thy conquering breath: 'tis stronger far
Than gun-powder or garlic.[15]

The removal of Corax's mask, however, immediately prompts Meleander to another outburst of temper, this time against hypocrisy and politicians; for the use of the mask has suggested simulation and deceit. Finally, by clever turns of dialogue, Corax creates an opportunity to mention a long-lost daughter; this remark strikes home; immediately the revived impetus of the old man's choleric disposition subsides. Dreaded melancholy paralyzes, then dissipates the comparatively objective frame of mind that the other humors— choler and the sanguine—had temporarily permitted him. He observes:

Cruel man!
How canst thou rip a heart that's cleft already
With injuries of time?—Whilst I am frantic,
Whilst throngs of rude divisions huddle on,
And so disrank my brains from peace and sleep,
So long—I am insensible of cares.[16]

In other words, his melancholic disposition is no more than melancholy, not madness; once provoked, it painfully restores the enfeebled old lord to the sanity that he dreads. The other humors, when active, have provided a refuge of objective fantasies; but melancholy is the hell, the "close-griping" and inescapable "hell . . . within his bosom." Ford, with customary logic, has emphasized the Elizabethan and Jacobean viewpoint; as Burton reminds us, it was better to be mad and go to Bedlam than to suffer the excess of melancholy, which was considered the most dreaded of the humors.

We are informed by Bright and Burton that natural melancholy was both dry and cold; that it produced sluggishness, solitariness, and despair. When within the clutches of his rooted melancholic humor, Meleander behaves according to theory almost precisely; it is the active interference of his choleric humor that apparently upsets the consistency of his behavior. But, as the reader has already observed, the paradox is extremely logical. In marked contrast to the cause of his melancholy, it is the hypocrisy of political motives that has seriously aggravated Meleander's choleric disposition, which in turn expends itself against the deceit of politicians. Actually, as we have seen, it serves as an antidote to his melancholic humor.

The physician Corax, who ministers to Meleander, is likewise typically Burtonian; throughout the play, he analyzes symptoms and prepares cures. Ford, by the footnote quoted above, has let us know that a major source of the conscientious doctor's knowledge is Burton's *Anatomy*. Consequently, once Corax has determined the causes of Meleander's distraction, he immediately, following Burtonian precepts, sets about the cure of it. He administers a sleeping potion. When awakened to music, a treatment strongly recommended by Burton, the long-suffering Meleander, who is innately skeptical of reality, at first asks to be allowed to "dream my dream out." But Corax will not permit it. "Morrow to your lordship!" he welcomes. "You took a jolly nap, and slept it soundly." Meleander, not only fearful of reality, but also suspicious of the well-intentioned motives of others, remains sardonically incredulous; he advises Corax to "study to gull the wise," but to leave him alone. One by one, however, the good tidings come in the name of Prince Palador— old honors restored, new offices tendered. But it is not his public honors so much, but rather the restoration of his daughter Eroclea that fully reëstablishes Meleander's health of mind, at least so far as his advanced age permits.

In arranging to restore both honors and daughter to Meleander, Corax recognized, as he also did in his treatment of Palador, a fundamental and highly sensible precept: to wit, the essential objective of the physician was not the correction of the humor, but rather the removal of the cause (or causes) of the humor's aggravation. Corax had, in an earlier passage, observed of Meleander:

> 'Twas a prince's tyranny
> Caused his distraction; and a prince's sweetness
> Must qualify that tempest of his mind.[17]

Somewhat more important than the analysis of Meleander to an understanding of Ford's refinement of psychiatric interpretations are his major studies in both love-melancholy and insane jealousy. In every instance, causes, motivations, and symptoms are exhaustively analyzed; action, where its potentialities are inevitable, is deliberately withheld until the emotional content is so strong that the passions can no longer be kept under restraint. From the introspective calm of the lovelorn Palador to the simmering fury of Giovanni, study and restraint are paramount. It is in this respect that Ford, depicting human emotion and behavior in fine detail and expertly established tones, refined both the Jacobean drama and, in particular, its use of madness.

Probably the most strictly Burtonian of all Ford's characters is Prince Palador in *The Lover's Melancholy*. Because of the fact that he is exactly cut to a pattern, he is also one of Ford's most uninteresting characters. Palador is so reticent, for example, that only the courtier Rhetias has guessed and understood the external cause of his melancholy. Others, however, are able to describe his symptoms more clearly. For example, Admetus advises us:

> He's the same melancholy man
> He was at his father's death; sometimes speaks sense
> But seldom mirth; will smile, but seldom laugh,
> Will lend an ear to business, deal in none;
> Gaze upon revels, antic fopperies,
> But is not moved; will sparingly discourse,
> Hear music; but what most he takes delight in
> Are handsome pictures.[18]

A little later, the physician Corax discovers the prince with a book:

A book! is this the early exercise
I did prescribe? instead of following health,
Which all men covet, you pursue disease.
Where's your great horse, your hounds, your set at tennis,
Your balloon-ball, the practice of your dancing,
Your casting of the sledge, or learning how
To toss a pike? all changed into a sonnet![19]

Burton had recognized two types of solitude: enforced, as in the scholar's case; voluntary, as in the case of imaginative and melancholic persons. He also had recognized that solitude invariably ends in troubled thoughts and irremediable melancholy; in brief, as Burton put it, in "willful self-destruction." Corax, following Burtonian precepts, which, for example, recommended a balance between study and exercise, with moderation in both, has deliberately attempted to entice the prince out of his voluntary habit of solitude and reflection by prescribing outdoor exercise and, of course, has failed. He now determines to uncover the root of the prince's melancholy, and arranges the masque of mad folk. Meanwhile, when the cause of the prince's distraction shall have been determined and the cure effected, Corax understandably resolves: "May rats gnaw all my books, if I get home once and come here again!"

The carefully prepared "Masque of Melancholy" results, as Corax intended, in the discovery of the cause of Palador's melancholy: frustrated love. But the masque itself and the six mad folk fail except to amuse the prince. An exhibition of love-melancholy has been deliberately left out: " 'Twas not in art," says Corax, "To personate the shadow of that fancy." A few moments later, he adds:

Love is the tyrant of the heart; it darkens
Reason, confounds discretion; deaf to counsel,
It runs a headlong course to desperate madness.[20]

"Hold!" commands the prince; "Let no man henceforth name

the word again," and immediately exits. Corax, ably tutored by Burton, has struck home; for Burton, affording a broad hint, wrote: "He that runs headlong from the top of a rock is not in so bad a case as he that falls into the gulf of love. For hence, saith Platina, comes Repentance, Dotage, they lose themselves, their wits, and make shipwreck of their fortunes altogether . . ."[21] Ford, following another Burtonian prescription, but a rather commonplace one—to wit, the only certain remedy for love-melancholy is to reunite the lovers—contrives the plot so that Eroclea shall be restored to the prince. Once this reunion is effected, Palador is cured.

The study of Palador is perhaps the most obvious example of Ford's scholarly genius and his consequent tendency toward the refinement of psychiatric interpretations. The result in this particular case is theatrically unfortunate. Palador is merely a few comparatively uninteresting pages of Burton given a body and permitted to ambulate in the robes of a prince. Nearly our entire attention is focused upon the pathological analysis of natural melancholy, which, unsupported by any more strenuous passion, is, along with phlegm, the dullest of the humors. Action has—for the moment, at least—ceased to be a theatrical medium. There is little movement, no protagonist, no serious emotional conflict. Indeed, Ford, in correcting the unrestraint of his predecessors, went too far in the right direction; in his next three plays he was to make the compromise between vigorous character and plot conception, on the one hand, and his inherent intellectual restraint, on the other, much more successful. In the delineation of Penthea, for one example, even though his habit of restraint remained predominant, Ford was to create a masterpiece that is only, and then rarely, surpassed by Shakespeare.

However restrained the portrait of Penthea, we cannot argue, as in the case of Palador, that her character interpretation is altogether static or without progression. To use G. F. Sensabaugh's phrase, she "droops to her grave, a victim of love-melancholy." When we first meet her, she is already a victim of melancholy; but she immediately enlists our admiration by rising through sheer force of character above both the grief and the temptations resulting from her unfortunate marriage. Unlike several of Ford's other characters, she is not a neo-Platonist; honor is her paramount virtue, and she refuses to accept the seventeenth-century neo-Platonic precept that true love is more important than marriage. She orders her lover Orgilus from her presence and, after he is gone, observes:

> Honour,
> How much we fight with weakness to preserve thee.[22]

So abhorrent to her is her marriage to the jealous and elderly Bassanes, that her resolution of chastity, the obligation of maintaining her marriage at any cost, seriously strains her emotional stability even before circumstances make this resolution a direct cause of her mental disintegration. The immediate provocation to her madness, however, is the irrationally jealous outburst of her husband Bassanes, who, fabricating monstrous fictions in his diseased mind, accuses her and her brother Ithocles of incest. From this point on, even the moral resolution of maintaining her marriage is barred to her; her strict sense of conventionality, meanwhile, cannot permit her to return to her lover, Orgilus. Ford, already having proved the disaster of unbridled individualism in 'Tis Pity She's A Whore, makes Penthea the martyr of social conformity; when, through circumstances the young wife, already emotionally weakened, can no longer maintain her marriage and thus conform to the dictums of society, she resolves to die. But Penthea, unlike Annabella and Giovanni, dies beautifully and makes her martyrdom far more appealing than that of the libertine brother and sister.

Once Penthea has resolved upon death and her mind starts to disintegrate, her inherent nobility becomes even more evident. She makes the princess Calantha her executrix and wills her brother

Ithocles to Calantha "in holiest rites of love," despite the fact that he had forced her marriage to Bassanes and she had little reason to extend such a favor:

> I must leave the world
> To revel in Elysium, and 'tis just
> To wish my brother some advantage here.[23]

This beautiful gesture, indicating her voluntary forgiveness of an injury that had led to her ruin, forever endears Penthea to the reader; of all Ford's characters, if not of all Jacobean characters, she most commands the reader's sympathy.

In her final appearance Penthea, apathetically resigned to her fate, is already insane. However, Ford, unable to emancipate himself entirely from logic, weaves a trace of reason into her final speeches:

> Sure, if we were all Sirens, we should sing pitifully,
> And 'twere a comely music, when in parts
> One sung another's knell . . .
> .   .   .   .
> . . . 'tis a fine deceit
> To pass away in a dream! indeed, I've slept
> With mine eyes open a great while. No falsehood
> Equals a broken faith; there's not a hair
> . . . but . . .
> . . . sinks me to the grave: I must creep thither;
> The journey is not long.

She talks of the many "prattling babes" she might have had, and thus tenderly suggests that perhaps children might have saved her marriage. Then she takes her lover Orgilus's hand:

> I'll kiss it;
> O, 'tis a fine soft palm!—hark, in thine ear,
> Like whom do I look, prithee? . . .
> Goodness! we had been happy . . .
> .   .   .   .

. . . Remember,
When we last gathered roses in the garden,
I found my wits; but truly you lost yours.[24]

If, in all literature, any lovelorn maiden is entitled to pine away
and die, Penthea seems to have that right; her emotional frustration and subsequent apathy both of mind and of spirit are certainly
more fully explained than those of any other frustrated person in
Jacobean drama. But the rationalistic Ford must always make cause
proportionally greater than effect; he must always exhaust the
potentialities of his study before we see the result. Consequently, by
Ford's invention, Penthea, as if psychopathic causes were not sufficient, resolves to starve herself to death and, of course, succeeds.
But, in dying, even from starvation, she dies beautifully. Her maid
tells us:

> She called for music,
> And begged some gentle voice to tune a farewell
> To life and griefs: Christalla touched the lute;
> I wept the funeral song.[25]

We are then told that she drew down "her veil, so died."

Despite all of Ford's logic, there is occasionally a touch of Keats
in him—a sensuous feeling for the beautiful expression. But more
important to the purpose of this chapter is his perfect, almost too
perfect, logic in depicting the causes and symptoms of madness.
Let us recall Aspatia of *The Maid's Tragedy* for a moment. In many
ways, indeed in most respects, her frustrated love, with its subsequent dotage, is similar to Penthea's melancholy and is as beautifully
delineated. They are twin sisters, so to speak, rocked in the same
cradle of adversity, and the song that the poet sings over them
is the same beautiful prelude to death. But we remember what
happened to Aspatia; unable to die, probably because Beaumont or
Fletcher had other plans for her, she was preserved, somewhat incongruously, for the melodramatic climax of the play. The credibil-

ity and logic of a plausible death were discarded in favor of stage device; the result was that Aspatia in the end became primarily a theatrical puppet of the playwright. Ford, on the contrary, left no doubt as to the plausibility of his heroine's manner of death; once there is sufficient cause for it, there is nothing very melodramatic about starvation. Even though he was at times compelled to make professional compromises, Ford, when he made them, generally made them wisely; and in Penthea's case, as in the entire play of *The Broken Heart,* he was much more interested in dramatic integrity than in melodramatic spectacle. Penthea, exhaustively analyzed without loss of spiritual vitality, is further testimony to Ford's characteristic restraint in depicting psychiatric subjects. Her progression from sanity to insanity is deliberate and studied; she is held before our imagination like a beautiful and gently wind-blown tapestry of pastel colorings, and finally, like a half-remembered autumn sunset, she and her griefs disintegrate.

Ford was rarely more dependent upon Burton than in the delineation of heroic jealousy. The playwright apparently recognized, as had Burton, two alternative courses that resulted from the frustration of love: either a rooted habit of melancholy, as in the cases of Palador and Penthea, or insane jealousy. The former alternative, as a rule, had little dramatic potentiality beyond itself; the latter, however, was or could be supercharged with theatrical dynamite. Consequently, interpretations of jealousy that led to an insane outburst served Ford for two purposes: they made, first of all, excellent pathological studies; second, they could dependably motivate a spectacular climax. Best of all, the primary purpose, if the distraught character was extensively analyzed, always justified the second or professional purpose. Dramatically, from Ford's viewpoint, nothing could be better; such studies afforded an effective balance between intellectual restraint and analysis, on the one hand, and, on the other, the spectacle so dear to the contemporary audience.

The plot of *Love's Sacrifice* is almost identical with that of Massinger's *Duke of Milan;* the treatment, and particularly the handling of the characters, is infinitely better. If Ford's insight into character was comparatively limited, it was at least more perceptive than Massinger's; secondly, Ford never lets his plot degenerate into melodrama without reason and, once melodrama is the logical result of the actions of distraught personalities, it ceases to be strictly melodrama. As was Ford's custom, the climactic spectacles of *Love's Sacrifice* are solidly and logically prepared for. Furthermore, the characters are not mere puppets of the plot. Unlike Sforza in the *Duke of Milan,* Ford's Philippo, duke of Pavia, is in the first place neither an abnormal libertine, nor, once he learns his wife is an adulteress, is he prompted to immediate revenge. As with many of Ford's characters, a habit of reflection is evident. Although he is inflamed to extreme jealousy by the report of his wife's adultery, the duke is also, after a short outburst, motivated by inherent logic to seeking proof, with the result that his fury is partially curbed:

The icy current of my frozen blood
Is kindled up in agonies as hot
As flames of burning sulphur. O my fate!
A cuckold! . . .
.   .   .   .
. . . Death above utterance!
Take heed you prove this true.[26]

His reason temporarily prevails over his passion. He insists upon proof. When his sister Fiormonda, scornful of the duchess Bianca's low birth, and her henchman D'Avolos goad him unmercifully, the latter even reminding him that he is "sure to have a bastard," the duke's jealous outbursts are still persistently tempered by a resolution of obtaining firsthand evidence. But, once he is an eyewitness to the apparent adultery of Bianca and Fernando, his jealousy nearly, but not quite, snuffs out the last vestige of sanity. With drawn sword he confronts Bianca, and when she asks, "What would you do now, pray?" he responds:

> What! shameless harlot!
> Rip up the cradle of thy cursed womb,
> In which the mixture of that traitor's lust
> Imposthumes for a birth of bastardy![27]

Yet, despite almost uncontrollable passion, he is restrained from immediate execution of revenge by his settled habit of reflection; and it is only the ruthless prompting of Fiormonda, calling him "faint coward," reminding him of "thy glorious ancestors," that ultimately steels him to the murder of his wife. Immediately, "hot in blood," to use his own phrase, he sets out after Fernando, whom he confronts with sword in one hand, bloody dagger in the other. But again, despite impassioned speech, his innate sensibility prevents immediate action; he insists that Fernando defend himself with his sword and before the scene ends he has been convinced of Bianca's chastity. Cursing "the fury of some hellish rage," he is crushed with remorse and self-pity:

> Whither now
> Shall I run from the day, where never man
> Nor eye, nor eye of Heaven may see a dog
> So hateful as I am?[28]

Remorse and a habit of melancholy give emphasis to Philippo's deep sense of conscience and produce the motives that eventually lead to his self-destruction. He is unable to "outlive" his own "outrage." As expected, he dies by his own hand and joins Bianca and Fernando, who has just poisoned himself, in the "triple tomb."

Not only, despite the duke's impassioned outbursts, is Ford's characteristically perceptive analysis of inner motives evident, but also, almost at every turn, Ford has indicated his debt to Burton. The duke, for example, has married the unknown Bianca primarily for her great beauty; Burton, as a precaution against jealousy and the causes of jealousy, had more than once advocated the choosing of a chaste rather than a beautiful wife. "Nay," wrote Burton, speaking of the unwise susceptibility to beauty, "Kings themselves I say will do it, and voluntarily submit their sovereignty to a lovely woman."[29] He had further insisted upon marriage according to position, age, and family. The duke, however, with possibly one exception, has broken all these precepts in marrying Bianca. Furthermore, the duke's jealousy conforms almost precisely to Burtonian pattern. "Those which are jealous," wrote Burton, "most part, if they be not otherwise relieved, proceed from suspicion to hatred, from hatred to frenzy, madness, injury, murder, and despair," adding a moment later, "In their madness many times, saith Vives, they make away themselves and others."[30] Elsewhere, it should be added, Burton specifically warned a husband against permitting a young and handsome man too easy access to his wife. The duke, in granting Fernando all but "the name of husband and . . . our bed," directly violates this sensible precept. Ironically enough, he is the victim of his own self-assured and egotistical confidence.

Bassanes in *The Broken Heart* is a far more complex study of jealousy than is the Duke of Pavia; yet, despite the complexity of his behavior, he is even more Burtonian. Unlike Philippo, he does not suffer from an excess of confidence in his wife's loyalty. On the contrary, as far as marital circumstances are concerned, he is the victim of a marked inferiority complex, a complex that results from his elderly age and apparent sexual impotence.[31] Knowing his distrust of women, the reader wonders why Bassanes had married at all. In accordance with an extreme symptom of jealousy noted by Burton, the nobleman makes his wife a prisoner in his house.[32] Furthermore, he is so preoccupied by his suspicions that he orders the window next the street "dammed up" lest Penthea should court "a gazer's glances." Burton had, for example, given especial emphasis to the theory that the eyes were the most certain messengers of love; he had spoken of their "spiritual vapors" that infect and bewitch the object. Ford was unquestionably mindful of this fundamental precept, for the emotionally strained Bassanes philosophizes:

> There's a lust
> Committed by the eye, that sweats and travails,
> . . . till the deformed bear-whelp,
> Adultery, be licked into the act,
> The very act: that light [the window] shall be dammed up;
> D'ye hear, sir?[33]

So obsessed is Bassanes by his ungrounded jealousy that marriage to him is a full-time labor of acting as warden to his wife. Concluding his present tirade, he summarizes his emotional instability with pregnant succinctness:

> Swarms of confusion huddle in my thoughts
> In rare distemper.—Beauty! O, it is
> An unmatched blessing or a horrid curse.[34]

When his wife's brother Ithocles requests a private audience with Penthea, Bassanes, whose mind has already shown signs of derangement, suspects incest, and observes to himself:

> Alone! Alone! what means that word "alone?"
> Why might not I be there?—hum!—he's her brother.
> Brothers and sisters are but flesh and blood,
> And this same whoreson court-ease is temptation
> To a rebellion in the veins.[35]

This passage, notably the phrase "whoreson court-ease," suggests another Burtonian precept. "Idleness," Burton had written, "overthrows all; in the empty heart love reigns, love tyrannizeth in an idle person."[36] Ironically, however, Bassanes himself is more a victim of idleness than is anybody else in the play; if he had had some definite job to do, his imagination undoubtedly would not have been a main cause of the "rebellion" in his own veins—a rebellion that, because of a sense of frustrated eroticism, has resulted in unjustified and almost unparalleled jealousy.

In all of Ford's interpretations, jealousy, once aroused, immediately provokes the choleric humor; not one of his "green-eyed" characters goes off to mope in a corner; quite on the contrary, it is the adustion of choler that underlies and motivates the temporary insanity of their jealous disposition. Such a pathological interpretation is strictly Burtonian. "Of all passions," wrote Burton, "Love is most violent, and of those bitter potions which this Love-Melancholy affords, this bastard Jealousy is the greatest"; and, speaking of jealousy, he continued, " 'Tis a more vehement passion, a more furious perturbation . . . a *gall* corrupting the honey of our life, madness, vertigo, plague, hell . . ."[37] In other words, choler, according to Burton, is the correlate of the jealous mind. Bassanes, a far more intricate study than the Duke of Pavia, not only precisely embodies with marked emphasis the theory just quoted, but his conduct also closely parallels a much more specific Burtonian pattern. "He will . . . swear and belie," wrote Burton of the victim of jealousy, "slander any man, curse, threaten, brawl, scold, fight; and sometimes again flatter and speak fair, ask forgiveness . . . condemn his rashness and folly, vow, protest, and swear he will never do so again."[38] Even prior to Bassanes' climactic outrage upon Ithocles, which immediately provokes his repentance, he can, despite his choleric humor and when it is to his advantage, "flatter and speak fair." He can, for example, abruptly turn from scolding the nurse Grausis to the courteous flattery of his fellow courtiers:

Most welcome, Prophilus; ladies and gentlemen,
To all my heart is open; you all honour me,—

. . . .

    (*Aside*) How they flutter,
Wagtails and jays together.[39]

Bit by bit, Bassanes' diseased imagination, for there is no justifiable cause for his suspicions, has been fanned by the inherent passions of jealousy to the explosion point. In a white heat of anger, he storms into the private chamber where Ithocles and Penthea are in conference:

I can forbear no longer; more, I will not:
Keep off your hands or fall upon my point.[40]

When he accuses brother and sister of "incest," Ithocles cries, "Monster!" and draws his sword. The possibly fatal duel is averted only by Penthea's intervention.

Burton, as quoted above, had written: "He will . . . condemn his rashness and folly, vow, protest, and swear he will never do so again." Bassanes, once he is shocked by the conviction that Penthea is innocent, follows this pathological precept not only to the letter, but almost to the final dot of an *i*. At the initial shock, when humiliation first cools off the white heat of his temporary insanity, Bassanes merely swears "some way . . . to outdo art." But, later, he is not only a devotee of penitence, but rationalization has also made him a student of "patience," as if, and this is certainly true of Bassanes, self-restraint was not a component part of his nature. Indeed, his inherent sensibility, a trait that is characteristic of Ford's psychiatric studies, impels him almost instinctively to the conventionality of penitence; but only patience, the very virtue that is farthest from his reach, can in his own judgment atone for the sin of his outrage upon Ithocles and consequently justify his penitence. The result is that, as far as patience is concerned, he becomes a calculating logician:

But, to redeem a sacrilege so impious,
Humility shall pour, before the deities
I have incensed, a largess of more patience
Than their displeased altars can require:
No tempests of commotion shall disquiet
The calms of my composure.[41]

A few moments later, tormented by the impetuous anger of Orgilus, Bassanes is a little more prosaic, equally resolved—but, above all, the student of patience and the difficulty of his effort are paramount:

> What a fool am I
> To bandy passion! ere I'll speak a word,
> I will look on and burst.[42]

Bassanes' struggle to regain his self-respect is a difficult one; but, in the end, as the direct result of his inborn sensibility and a painstaking logic that is typical of several of Ford's characters, this fundamentally good man succeeds in overcoming his own inherent weaknesses. Well deserved, one feels, is his appointment as "Sparta's marshal."

II

The foregoing analyses of mad folk reflect, time and again, varied principles of contemporary psychopathology. Moreover, unlike the characterizations of Shakespeare and Webster, Ford's psychiatric studies present few undertones and irregularities; almost their every action and word can be explained by theory. Consequently, a careful examination of them substantially supports the hypothesis that Ford, notwithstanding an inherent faith in the nobility of man, was basically a theorist, and not an instinctive interpreter, of psychopathic processes. Burton's comprehensive and currently popular *The Anatomy of Melancholy* was the most likely source book of both the student of psychiatry and the academically minded playwright of Ford's time. There are, as I have noted in an earlier chapter, strong indications that Massinger, in both *The Duke of Milan* and *The Very Woman,* was dependent on Burton's work. But Massinger had no abiding interest in psychiatric studies except in so far as they could motivate a plot that was riddled with spectacular episodes. Like Fletcher, he was primarily a playwright, and not a student of human nature. The scholarly Ford, on the other hand, was not only persistently interested in problems of human conduct, but, lacking the natural insight that typifies the character conceptions of Shakespeare and Webster, he appears to have looked to the printed page, and not to life, for his understanding of the many and variable psychoses that determine human behavior. His debt to Burton was acknowledged early (in *The Lover's Melancholy*); and so typically Burtonian are not only his important psychiatric interpretations, but also, as I have noted, their (and others') repeated observations concerning abnormal human conduct that there can be very little doubt that these characters were conceived—and, to a large extent, elucidated upon—from the pages of Burton's *Anatomy*.

In addition to this dependence upon theory, Ford's own character and, particularly, its scholarly habit of logic are evidenced time and again by the behavior and the sentiments of his mad folk. Apart from, and sometimes despite, their deranged minds, his mad folk are unusually rational. Penthea's melancholy and subsequent insanity, are, for example, the direct result of the predominant attribute of reason that compels her to place conformity to convention above the instincts of nature. Philippo's half-crazed impulses, for another example, are repeatedly thwarted by his ingrained habit of reflection; and Bassanes, as we have noted, becomes a logician who seeks to destroy his baser and animal instincts by the sheer power of reason. Also, each of these mad folk, as well as Palador, reveals a high degree of sensibility, that is, a delicate awareness that distinguishes between what is right and what is wrong. It is this quality —the quality of sensibility—that gives to Ford's plays a very high tone of morality.

If what I have said is true, how can the rather shocking plot of *'Tis Pity She's A Whore* be justified by the preceding standards? Can it be termed a rational, if not a moralistic, play? How, if at all, is it typical of Ford's work? The answer seems to be that *'Tis Pity* is typical of Ford only if we look at the moral argument of the play in reverse. Giovanni, in the beginning, is a young man of both sensibility and logic, even though these two human attributes are soon to be divided and pitted against each other. He at first, for example, consults Friar Bonaventura only because he is horrified at his abnormal passion for his sister; but, almost immediately, his powers of logic are turned against his innate awareness of what is right and, with careful arguments, he attempts to prove that his unnatural passion is a moral one. Little by little, as his distinction between what is morally right and what morally wrong disintegrates, Giovanni becomes, as Ford seems to have intended, something of a monstrosity; the human attribute of reason, which normally should abet the dictates of conscience, is repeatedly called upon to defend the amorality of the beast. His rationalizations, moreover, are so convincing to him that Giovanni can eventually indulge in incest and its worship not only without the slightest qualm of conscience, but also with exultation. Ford, through the forcible rectitude and logic of Father Bonaventura, quite obviously disapproves of him; and his final purpose in depicting Giovanni is to show that the amoral omnipotence of bestial instincts, once the sensibility of the human conscience has been displaced, will also, in the end, utterly destroy the heterogeneous and progressively weakened powers of reason. Hence, it is Giovanni, who has become more beast than man, that embarks on the ultimate and irrational slaughter.

Ford's thesis of human conduct as it is presented in *'Tis Pity* seems, therefore, to differ little from that of the other plays. If, in *The Broken Heart*, Ford has shown us that a man can rehabilitate himself through an abiding awareness of right conduct when this awareness is supported forcibly by the use of logic, he also, in the study of Giovanni, shows us the tragedy attendant upon the opposite course of conduct. To Ford, man was a highly rational creature of marked sensibility. If anything less, if in particular he should lose his perspective of right and wrong, he ceased, according to the degree of his deficiency, to deserve approval as the full and complete human being.

At the beginning of this chapter I made the statement that Ford, by restoring the emphasis to character study, created mad folk that are considerably more reminiscent of those of Shakespeare and Webster than akin to those of his immediate predecessors. In contrast to the poorly explained psychotic characters that we find in Fletcher's and Massinger's tragedies, not only the very evident moral perspective, but also the causes and symptoms of Ford's psychiatric portrayals are, as we have noted, carefully and exhaustively analyzed. This analysis, moreover, is invariably more complete and, with the exception of Giovanni,[43] more pronouncedly emphasized than the presentation of the spectacle that sometimes evolves from the conduct of the mad folk. It is in this respect that Ford, by the analysis and refinement of psychiatric studies, made his most marked departure from the traditional use of mad folk and distraught characters as it had been developed in the latter half of the Jacobean period. Fletcher and Massinger had been interested almost exclusively in the theatrical exploitation of mentally abnormal characters and had used them primarily as mediums of spectacle. So long as these playwrights could please their audiences with melodramatic episodes, they (and particularly Fletcher) cared very little about the veracity of their character portrayals—in fact, so little that it is sometimes difficult to determine what particular psychoses underlie the behavior. Ford, on the other hand, by constantly probing and interpreting psychological motives and, when necessary, consulting Burton, created characters that, as theoretical interpretations of human conduct, not only follow carefully prepared patterns of behavior, but are invariably more important than the theatrical spectacle which, when presented, is the natural result of the carefully analyzed motives. In this sense, he helped to check the course of a theater that, at the moment, was verging upon outright melodrama. More-over, by returning the emphasis to character study, particularly in his interpretations of mad folk, Ford added a much-needed aura of dignity to the closing years of Jacobean tragedy.

Even though, in the thorough analysis of character, Ford is remi-niscent of both Shakespeare and Webster, he quite evidently was far from directly influenced by either the moral outlook or the technique of the earlier Jacobeans. Indeed, his psychiatric studies differ in at least three fundamental respects from those of Shake-speare, Webster, and their contemporaries. The first difference is primarily a moral one. Madmen, particularly during the first decade of the Jacobean period, in reflecting the very evident skepticism of the playwright, had been portrayed by their authors as embodiments either of human insignificance or of moral degeneration; they and their distraught brethren, together with the social background from which they evolved, were mediums through which the early play-wrights, such as Shakespeare, Tourneur, and Webster, studied and expostulated upon both the futility and the evil of mankind. Several of them, such as Macbeth, D'Amville, and Ferdinand, are brought to insanity because of their own evil. Others, who are good people, such as Cornelia, are driven to madness by the environment of wickedness in which they have become ensnared. But all, or almost all, attest either to the futility or to the evil of human society. In contrast to these early mad folk, those of Ford reflect very little of the immanent and pervasive skepticism that had characterized the tragedy of the first decade of the period. In the first place, differing markedly from most of his early predecessors, Ford does not pre-sent a single psychopathic study of a person who is basically evil; indeed, all of Ford's mad folk, except Giovanni, are unusually good and highly moral people, and Giovanni's moral evil is the unfortu-nate result, and not a cause, of the abnormality over which he has little or no control. Further, in perhaps equal contrast to the tragic

drama not only of Shakespeare's time, but of the entire period, all
of Ford's mental cases, with the exceptions of Giovanni and Philippo,
are members of societies in which there is hardly a trace of moral
or political evil. In Philippo's case, moreover, the essentially good
people of the play, particularly Bianca and Fernando, are much
more important than the evil ones; similarly, in *'Tis Pity,* the petty
intriguers that infiltrate into the plot are completely overshadowed
by Father Bonaventura, who, as a bulwark of rectitude, appears to
represent Ford's evident confidence in the fundamental goodness
of mankind.

A second basic distinction to Ford's treatment of mad folk is
evidenced by his strong and optimistic faith in their destiny, be it
a complete rehabilitation in this world or a better life in the next.
When we review the earlier mad folk of the Jacobean period, it is
difficult, except in comedy or farce, to find a single one who survives
his distraction. Furthermore, in dying, the great majority, we discover, fail to envision a better life beyond; and some, moreover,
deliberately voice their disillusionment not only in mankind, but
also in the promise of any world to come.[44] It is noteworthy, first
of all, that three of Ford's mad folk—Palador, Meleander, and Bassanes, each one a serious study—not only survive the prolonged
onslaught of their madness, but also are restored to happier and
more worthwhile lives than they had previously experienced. Also,
in equally marked contrast to the general pessimism early in the
period, each of Ford's mad folk or distraught characters who dies
expresses, in dying, either a high moral sentiment or confidence in
a happier existence in the next world. Giovanni's comment, however, must in this respect be considered with some reservation; his
optimistic hope of again embracing Annabella expresses primarily
his own personal confidence and not necessarily Ford's faith that a
better world awaits him. But Penthea, as we know, departs "to
revel in Elysium"; and Philippo ennobles his own death by refusing

to outlive his "outrage" and, furthermore, in dying, he envisions his reunion with Bianca.

Ford, therefore, although he is most like Shakespeare and Webster in that he placed the emphasis of tragedy upon character interpretation, differs very markedly, on the other hand, from the early Jacobean playwright in his psychological outlook. Mad folk to Ford were not the symbols of man's disillusionment, and, consequently, were not necessarily doomed to death and to possible nihilism. As far as he was concerned, their troubles neither originated from the black wickedness of man, nor reflected it. Ford's interest in the use of madness was, in contrast to that of Shakespeare and Webster, influenced by neither moral nor philosophical considerations; it was almost purely a scientific interest, which was undoubtedly encouraged by the fact that mad folk were highly popular stage devices. Ford was writing at a time when Jacobean skepticism had more or less expended itself; he was not particularly concerned with what was morally wrong with man. On the contrary, he was interested primarily, from a detached and scholarly viewpoint, in psychopathic phenomena and their causes.

In his objective and abiding interest in psychopathology, Ford is unique among the successful Jacobean tragic playwrights. It can be argued, of course, that the psychological interpretations of Shakespeare, Webster, Fletcher, Massinger, and others reflect their author's awareness of many contemporary theories about madness; but none of these playwrights, if we overlook Jonson, who was interested in behavior rather than psychopathic principles, can be considered slavishly indebted to theory. They either, as Shakespeare and Webster did, resorted largely to instinctive insight in depicting the finer detail of mad folk, and in such case the playwright's insight was often sharpened by a deep sense of disillusionment; or, like Fletcher, they embodied a psychopathic theory or two in a distraught character for the purpose of using him, often incongruously, as an instrument of theatricality. Ford's technique, by contrast, was that of a pains-taking student of psychiatry, one whose primary interest lies in mad-ness itself. With the possible exception of his study of Penthea, his reliance on theory is invariably paramount; and, even in Penthea's case, the general outline of her mental disintegration accords very closely with Burton's theories of love-melancholy. In marked con-trast to the inspired geniuses of Shakespeare and Webster, Ford was primarily a technician; his characters basically are mechanical embodiments of theory. But some of them, paradoxically, are more than that; they breathe and have life. Ford, although fundamentally a technician, also possessed a quiet and ennobling faith in human qualities, particularly in human sensibility. It is this faith—so un-usual in the technician—that, enriching several of Ford's characters, gives them warmth and humanity.

NOTES

BIBLIOGRAPHY

INDEX

NOTES

1 Bethlehem Hospital and Its Background

1. Bucknill, *The Mad Folk of Shakespeare* (2nd ed.; London, 1867).
2. Somerville, *Madness in Shakespearean Tragedy* (London, 1929).
3. Campbell, "What Is The Matter With Hamlet," *The Yale Review*, XXXII (1942), 309–322.
4. Jones, "A Psycho-Analytic Study of Hamlet," *Essays in Applied Psycho-Analysis* (London, 1922), pp. 1–98.
5. Dr. Daniel Hack Tuke, *Chapters in the History of the Insane in the British Isles* (London, 1882). Dr. James J. Walsh, "Nursing the Insane and Feeble-minded," in *The History of Nursing* (New York, 1929).
6. Tuke, p. 1 ff.
7. *Ibid.*, p. 7.
8. *Ibid.*, p. 14.
9. *Ibid.*, p. 29.
10. Stow, *A Survey of London* (1603), ed. by C. L. Kingsford (Oxford, 1908), vol. II, p. 98 and p. 143, respectively.
11. *State Papers Domestic,* Chas. I, 10 October 1632.
12. Stow, vol. II, p. 98.
13. Edward G. O'Donoghue, *The Story of Bethlehem Hospital From Its Foundation in 1247* (London, 1914), p. 69. O'Donoghue, at the time he wrote this book, was chaplain of Bethlehem Hospital.
14. Henry VIII's charter, dated 13 January 1547, and the petition of 1538 for the control of Bethlehem by the city council of London are both included in the *Memoranda Relating to the Royal Hospitals of London* (London, 1836).
15. Knight, *Cyclopedia of London* (London, 1851), p. 355.
16. This extract, as quoted by Knight, also mentions "one messuage newly built . . . containing a cellar, a kitchen, a hall, four chambers, and a garret." There is no mention of what the four chambers were used for; possibly, but far from certainly, they were used as cells.
17. *State Papers Domestic,* Chas. I, 10 October 1632.
18. O'Donoghue, *The Story of Bethlehem Hospital,* p. 168; as quoted from an entry in the Court Books, 1631, in which a visit to the hospital by two governors of Bethlehem is reported.
19. *Memoranda Relating to the Royal Hospitals* (London, 1836).
20. *State Papers Domestic,* Chas. I, 10 October 1632.
21. In *Memoranda Relating to the Royal Hospitals,* Appendix pp. 116–117, there is published a royal grant dated 14 October 14 Car. I, 1638, which "conceded" Bethlehem to "said Mayor and commonalty of Citizens"; this wording indicates that James may have actually succeeded in illegally acquiring the ownership of the Hospital.

22. *State Papers Domestic,* Chas. I, 10 October 1632. According to the report, the "casual gifts" consisted mainly of food. The steward sold these "gifts" to patients at "excessive rates."

23. O'Donoghue, *The Story of Bethlehem Hospital,* p. 156.

24. *State Papers Domestic,* James 1, 10 December 1618.

25. *Remembrancia* (London, 1878). *Remembrancia* is a collection of old documents that was published by the city government of London in 1878. The particular document (written 1622) from which I make this general conclusion, and which is a statement by the president and governors of Bethlehem, not only tells that the hospital was unable to meet its expenses, but also that it must depend upon "the gifts of many well affected citizens." These gifts, which were accepted by the steward and sometimes sold at six times their value to the inmates, were generally limited to food, clothing, and drink. The hospital, particularly during Jacobean times, was apparently unable to provide its patients with the ordinary necessities of life.

26. O'Donoghue, *The Story of Bethlehem Hospital,* p. 182, as quoted from the Court Books (July 18, 1646).

27. Lupton, "London and the Countrey Carbonadoed" (1632), *The Aungervyle Society Publications,* 2nd ser., no. XV (Edinburgh, 1883), section on "Bedlam," pp. 25–26.

28. W. E. Campbell, ed., *The English Works of Sir Thomas More* (New York, 1931), vol. I, p. 461.

29. O'Donoghue, *The Story of Bethlehem Hospital,* p. 405. Quoted from Historical Mss., Report VI, part I, February 6, 1609–10: appendix p. 229b.

30. Jonson, *Bartholomew Fair,* act I, sc. 5; *Ben Jonson,* ed. by Herford and Simpson (Oxford, 1938), vol. VI, p. 32.

31. Jonson, *The Silent Woman,* act II, sc. 2; *ibid.,* vol. V, p. 179.

32. Middleton, *A Mad World, My Masters,* act V, sc. 2; *The Works of Thomas Middleton,* ed. by A. H. Bullen (London, 1885), vol. III, p. 357.

33. *As You Like It,* act III, sc. 2; *The Comedies of Shakespeare,* ed. by W. J. Craig (London, 1922), p. 711.

34. *The Roaring Girl,* act III, sc. 3; *The Works of Thomas Middleton,* ed. by A. H. Bullen (London, 1885), vol. IV, p. 83.

35. The court order of 1657 that closed the doors of Bethlehem on Sundays and certain holidays evolved out of the indiscreet plying of mad folk with liquor. (O'Donoghue, *The Story of Bethlehem Hospital,* pp. 182–183; quoted from Court Books of 1657, June 12th.)

36. Tom Brown, *London Amusements* (1700), ed. by Arthur L. Hayward (New York, 1927), p. 26 ff.

37. Edward Ward, *The London Spy,* issue of January 1699; as collected and published (London, 1703).

38. Brown; see note 36.

39. Ward; see note 37.

40. G. B. Harrison, ed., *A Second Elizabethan Journal* (New York, 1931), p. 27.

41. *State Papers Domestic,* James I, 8 May 1619.

42. *The Tatler,* no. CXXVII (January 31, 1709).

43. As Bright and Burton tell us, delusional insanity resulted from the adustion of melancholy. Burton, writing of the adustion of melancholy, said that the victims imagine "they are beasts, wolves, hogs . . . bray like asses." *The Anatomy of Melancholy* (1621), edited by Dell and Jordan-Smith (New York, 1941), part I, sec. 3, memb. 1, subsec. 3; p. 342.

44. See note 35.

45. *The Honest Whore; Northward Ho;* and *The Pilgrim.*

46. Dekker, *The Honest Whore,* part I, act V, sc. 2; *Thomas Dekker* (Mermaid Series, unexpurgated ed.; London, n.d.), p. 179.

47. John Stow, *A Survey of London,* as edited and enlarged upon by John Strype (6th ed., London, 1754), vol. I, p. 220.

48. Middleton and Rowley, *The Changeling,* act IV, sc. 3; *Typical Elizabethan Plays,* ed. by Schelling and Black (3rd ed.; New York, 1949), p. 838.

49. Lupton; see note 27.

50. Another indication that most inmates of asylums were considered curable is the statement by Stow, himself an Elizabethan, that the fourteenth-century hospital in Barking parish was founded "for poor Priests and other men and women that were sick of the Phrenzie, there to remain until they were . . . restored to good memory." *A Survey of London,* 1603 (Oxford, 1908), vol. II, p. 143.

51. Walsh; see note 5.

2   Bedlam and the Theater

1. Thomas Dekker, *The Honest Whore,* part I (1604), act V, sc. 2; *Thomas Dekker* (Mermaid Series, unexpurgated ed.; London, n.d.). This quotation and those following are from pp. 177 ff.

2. John Webster, *The Duchess of Malfi* (1614), act IV, sc. 2; *Typical Elizabethan Plays,* ed. by Schelling and Black (3rd ed.; New York, 1949), This quotation and those following are from pp. 790 ff.

3. Edward G. O'Donoghue, *The Story of Bethlehem Hospital From Its Foundation in 1247* (London, 1914), "Dr. Crooke," pp. 156 ff.

4. *State Papers Domestic,* Chas. I, 17 April 1633.

5. Thomas Middleton, *The Changeling* (*c.* 1622), act III, sc. 3; *Typical Elizabethan Plays,* ed. by Schelling and Black (3rd ed.; New York, 1949), p. 829.

6. *Ibid.,* p. 826.

7. John Fletcher, *The Pilgrim* (1621), act III, sc. 6; *The Works of*

Beaumont and Fletcher (London, 1840), vol. I. This quotation and those following are from pp. 603 ff.

8. King James had written in *Daemonologie* (1597) that "witches . . . make folkes to becom . . . maniacque"; *Daemonologie,* ed. by G. B. Harrison (London, 1924), p. 47.

9. In *The Mad Lover,* Fletcher refers to madness as "a gentleman-like humour, and in fashion" (act IV, sc. 1); *The Works of Francis Beaumont and John Fletcher* (variorum ed., London, 1908), vol. III, p. 186.

10. Beaumont and Fletcher, *The Nice Valour* (date uncertain), act III, sc. 3; *The Works of Beaumont and Fletcher* (London, 1866), vol. II, p. 464.

11. Robert Burton, *The Anatomy of Melancholy* (1621), ed. by Dell and Jordan-Smith (New York, 1941), part I, sec. 3, memb. 1, subsec. 2; pp. 328–329.

12. Fletcher, *The Noble Gentleman* (1625), act III, sc. 2; *The Works of Beaumont and Fletcher* (London, 1866), vol. II, p. 270.

13. I use the term "instruments of satire" to apply to persons when they make critical comments that do not bring ridicule upon themselves, but that are objectively directed at persons in other professions.

14. F. P. Wilson, *Elizabethan and Jacobean* (Oxford, 1946), p. 97.

3 The Theories of Mental Pathology and of Conduct

1. Vicary, *The Anatomie of the Bodie of Man* (1548) (Early English Text Society ed., London, 1888).

2. *Ibid.,* pp. 70–71.

3. *Ibid.,* p. 71.

4. *Ibid.,* pp. 71–72.

5. *Ibid.,* p. 70.

6. *Ibid.,* p. 62.

7. Robert Burton, *The Anatomy of Melancholy* (1621), part I, sec. 3, memb. 1, subsec. 3; ed. by Dell and Jordan-Smith (New York, 1941), pp. 339–340.

8. Bright, *A Treatise of Melancholie* (1586), The Facsimile Text (New York, 1940), chap. xvii, pp. 102 ff.

9. Bright devoted chap. xvi of *A Treatise of Melancholie* to an attempt to prove that the humors, by corrupting either the heart (the instrument of "affection") or the brain (the instrument of "apprehension"), are in themselves sufficient to occasion fairly pronounced passions, whether choleric or sanguine. However, he invariably reverts to the idea that an external cause, even though slight or misconceived, is prerequisite to the more extravagant manifestations of the passion.

10. Bright, chap. xvi, pp. 94–96.

11. *Hamlet,* act II, sc. 2; *The Tragedies of Shakespeare,* ed. by W. J. Craig (London, 1922), p. 671.

12. J. M. Guardia, *Essai Sur L'Ouvrage de Juan Huarte* (Paris, 1855), p. 4. Huarte's book was first translated into French in 1580, into Italian in 1582. Such was its influence that Guardia was able to write: "Il se répandait . . . dans toute L'Europe savante."

13. *Ibid.*, p. 57.

14. *Julius Caesar*, act V, sc. 5; *The Tragedies of Shakespeare*, ed. by W. J. Craig (London, 1922), p. 543.

15. For example, Donne (*An Anatomy of the World* in particular), Ralegh (notably, recurrent skepticism in *The History of The World*), Norden (*Vicissitudo Rerum*), Goodman (*The Fall of Man*), and most of the well-known playwrights predating Ford.

16. The Elizabethan translation of Machiavelli's *The Prince*, ed. by Hardin Craig (Chapel Hill: University of North Carolina Press, 1944).

17. *The Tragedy of Hoffman* (c. 1603), act II, sc. 1; ed. by A. F. Hopkinson (London, 1917), p. 22.

4   The Pathological Studies of Melancholy

1. For a critical analysis evaluating the influence of the breakdown of medieval concepts upon the Jacobean mind, see George Williamson, "Mutability, Decay, and Seventeenth Century Melancholy," *A Journal of English Literary History*, II (1935), 121–150.

2. Louise C. Turner Forest, "A Caveat for Critics against Invoking Elizabethan Psychology," *PMLA*, LXI (1946), pp. 651–672.

3. Burton, *The Anatomy of Melancholy* (1621), part I, sec. 3, memb. 1, subsec. 2; ed. by Dell and Jordan-Smith (New York, 1948), pp. 337–338.

4. Rhubarb was considered a good Elizabethan cure for choler. In *The White Devil*, Flamineo remarks to Marcello: "Are you choleric? I'll purge 't with rhubarb." Burton, in the *Anatomy*, said that "Rhubarb," although not "proper to this humour [melancholy]," was still a good remedy: "For, as Montaltus holds, and Montanus, choler is to be purged because it feeds the other." (*Anatomy*, part II, sec. 4, memb. 2, subsec. 3; p. 581.)

5. John Webster, *The Duchess of Malfi* (1614), act II, sc. 5; *Typical Elizabethan Plays*, ed. by Schelling and Black (3rd ed.; New York, 1949), p. 774.

6. *Ibid.*, act III, sc. 2; p. 779.

7. *Ibid.*, act IV, sc. 2; p. 794.

8. *Ibid.*, act V, sc. 2; p. 796.

9. *The Anatomy of Melancholy*, part I, sec. 3, memb. 1, subsec. 3; p. 342.

10. *Ibid.*, subsec. 2; p. 334.

11. *Ibid.*

12. Webster, *The Duchess of Malfi*, act V, sc. 5; p. 805.

13. Webster, *The White Devil* (1612), act I, sc. 2; *The Complete Works of John Webster*, ed. by F. L. Lucas (New York, 1937), p. 121.

14. *Ibid.*, act V, sc. 2; p. 171.

15. *Ibid.*, sc. 4; p. 181.

16. Beaumont and Fletcher, *The Maid's Tragedy* (c. 1610), act II, sc. 1; *Typical Elizabethan Plays*, ed. by Schelling and Black (3rd ed.; New York, 1949), p. 716.

17. Burton, *The Anatomy of Melancholy*, part III, sec. 2, memb. 4; p. 763.

18. Sigmund Freud, *A General Introduction to Psycho-Analysis* (New York, 1935), p. 268.

19. *Ibid.*, p. 270.

20. Fletcher and Shakespeare, *The Two Noble Kinsmen* (1613), act III, sc. 4; *The Complete Works of Shakespeare*, ed. by G. L. Kittredge (New York, 1936), p. 1429.

21. Both Ophelia and The Jailor's Daughter, although primarily victims of the adustion of melancholy, were by temperament phlegmatic characters. Burton, quoting Melancthon, was to write of persons suffering from pronounced conditions of phlegm: "They delight in waters, ponds, pools, rivers." (*Anatomy*, part I, sec. 3, memb. 1, subsec. 3; p. 340.)

22. Fletcher and Shakespeare, *The Two Noble Kinsmen*, act IV, sc. 1; p. 1437.

23. Philip Massinger, *The Very Woman* (1634), act II, sc. 3; *The Plays of Philip Massinger*, ed. by W. Gifford (3rd ed.; Baltimore, 1856), p. 445.

24. *Ibid.*, p. 446.

25. Burton, *The Anatomy of Melancholy*, part III, sec. 2, memb. 5, subsec. 1; pp. 774–775.

26. *Ibid.*, part III, sec. 2, memb. 4; p. 763.

27. Reginald Scot, *The Discovery of Witchcraft* (1584; London, 1665), p. 4.

28. Burton, *The Anatomy of Melancholy*, part I, sec. 3, memb. 1, subsec. 2; p. 328.

29. John Marston, *Antonio's Revenge* (1602), act IV, sc. 1; *The Works of John Marston*, ed. by A. H. Bullen (London, 1887), vol. I, pp. 157–158.

30. Webster, *The Duchess of Malfi*, act I, sc. 2; p. 763.

31. Webster, *The White Devil*, act V, sc. 3; p. 177.

32. Webster, *The Duchess of Malfi*, act I, sc. 2; pp. 762–763.

33. *Ibid.*, act V, sc. 2; p. 801.

34. *Ibid.*, act II, sc. 1; p. 767.

35. Marston, *Antonio's Revenge*, act III, sc. 1; p. 147.

5 The Theatricality of Near Madness

1. A list of humor characters whose abnormalities or cures are artificially manipulated by the playwright for the purpose of emphasizing

turns of plot and theatricality would include, among others, Dowsecer in Chapman's *A Humorous Day's Mirth;* the King in Dekker's *Match Me In London;* Follywit in Middleton's *A Mad World, My Masters;* among Fletcher's plays, Alphonso and Roderigo in *The Pilgrim,* Mirabel and Belleur in *The Wild Goose Chase,* the phlegmatic Leon in *Rule A Wife, Have A Wife,* and Memnon in *The Mad Lover;* among Massinger's plays, Luke and Lady Frugal in *The City Madam,* Almira and Cardenas in *The Very Woman,* and Theophilus in the tragedy *The Virgin Martyr.* Likewise, the reader will recall Fletcher's (or Beaumont's) treatment of The Passionate Lord; also we should not forget Fletcher's miraculous cure of The Jailor's Daughter, who, although a study in outright madness, typifies the artificiality with which Jacobean playwrights often treated their humor studies.

2. Lady Eleanor's *Strange and Wonderful Prophecies* was published under still another name, her maiden name Lady Eleanor Audley.

3. Most Tom O'Bedlams, like Pug, appear to have been imposters. In 1675 the governors of the hospital stated in a public notice: "Whereas several vagrant persons do wander about . . . pretending themselves to be lunatics, under care in the Hospital of Bethlem, with brass plates on their arms and inscriptions thereon; these are to give notice, that there is no such liberty given . . ., neither is any such plate as a distinction or mark put upon any lunatick during their time of being here or when discharged thence." Quoted from *London Gazette* 1000 by Tuke, *Chapters in the History of the Insane in the British Isles* (London, 1882).

4. Thomas Middleton, *A Trick To Catch The Old One* (*c.* 1606), act III, sc. 4; *The Works of Thomas Middleton,* ed. by A. H. Bullen (Boston, 1885), vol. II, p. 308.

5. John Fletcher, *The Pilgrim* (1621), act II, sc. 1; *The Works of Mr. Francis Beaumont and Mr. John Fletcher* (London, 1750), vol. V, p. 458.

6. *Ibid.,* act III, sc. 1; p. 474.

7. E. H. C. Oliphant, *The Plays of Beaumont and Fletcher* (New Haven, 1927), concludes that the *Nice Valour* was, for the most part, the draft of Beaumont, but that it was later extensively revised by Fletcher. He indicates, moreover, that the treatment of Shamont and, therefore, probably of Lapet was mostly Fletcher's work. Quite likely, most of the extravagance of character conception in the play was primarily the workmanship of Fletcher rather than that of the more restrained Beaumont.

8. These characters are, respectively, the chief motivators of plot in Fletcher's *Valentinian, The Bloody Brother,* and *The Double Marriage,* and in Massinger's *Unnatural Combat* and *Virgin Martyr.*

6 John Ford, and the Refinement of Bedlam

1. U. M. Ellis-Fermor, *The Jacobean Drama* (London, 1936), p. 235.
2. Produced at Blackfriars and Globe Theaters in 1628.

3. Robert Burton, *The Anatomy of Melancholy* (1621), part I, sec. 1, memb. 1, subsec. 4 (Everyman's Library, London, 1932), vol. I, p. 141.

4. John Ford, *The Lover's Melancholy* (1628), act III, sc. 3; *John Ford,* ed. by Havelock Ellis (Mermaid Series, London, n.d.), p. 55.

5. Burton, *The Anatomy of Melancholy* (Everyman's Library), vol. I, p. 142.

6. Ford, *The Lover's Melancholy,* act III, sc. 3; p. 55.

7. *Ibid.,* p. 56.

8. Burton, *The Anatomy of Melancholy,* part I, sec. 3, memb. 2, subsec. 2 (Everyman's Library), vol. I, p. 412.

9. Ford, *The Lover's Melancholy,* act III, sc. 3; p. 57.

10. *Ibid.,* p. 58.

11. *Ibid.,* act III, sc. 1, p. 44.

12. *Ibid.,* act II, sc. 2; p. 36.

13. *Ibid.,* p. 38.

14. *Ibid.,* act IV, sc. 2; p. 65.

15. *Ibid.*

16. *Ibid.,* p. 66.

17. *Ibid.,* p. 63.

18. *Ibid.,* act I, sc. 1; p. 10.

19. *Ibid.,* act II, sc. 1; p. 26.

20. *Ibid.,* act III, sc. 3; p. 58.

21. Burton, *The Anatomy of Melancholy,* part III, sec. 2, memb. 4 (Everyman's Library), vol. III, p. 186.

22. Ford, *The Broken Heart* (1633), act II, sc. 3; *John Ford,* ed. by Havelock Ellis (Mermaid Series, London, n.d.), p. 221.

23. *Ibid.,* act III, sc. 5; p. 243.

24. *Ibid.,* act IV, sc. 2; pp. 253–255.

25. *Ibid.,* act IV, sc. 4; p. 265.

26. Ford, *Love's Sacrifice* (1633), act III, sc. 3; *John Ford,* ed. by Havelock Ellis (Mermaid Series, London, n.d.), p. 340.

27. *Ibid.,* act V, sc. 1; p. 361.

28. *Ibid.,* act V, sc. 2; p. 368. For example, both Bright and Burton had observed that melancholics will fly society, flee to a wilderness.

29. Burton, *The Anatomy of Melancholy,* part III, sec. 2, memb. 2, subsec. 2 (Everyman's Library), vol. III, p. 68.

30. *Ibid.,* part III, sec. 3, memb. 3; vol. III, p. 286.

31. For example, Burton lists impotency in performing the sexual duties expected of a husband as a chief cause of jealousy. (*Anatomy,* part III, sec. 3, memb. 1, subsec. 2 (Everyman's Library), vol. III, pp. 266–267.

32. Burton had written: "They [jealous husbands] lock their wives still in their houses, which are so many prisons to them, will suffer nobody to come at them . . . . They must not so much as look out." *Anatomy,* part III, sec. 3, memb. 2 (Everyman's Library), vol. III, p. 283.

33. Ford, *The Broken Heart,* act II, sc. 1; p. 206.

34. *Ibid.*, p. 208.

35. *Ibid.*, act II, sc. 2; p. 216.

36. Burton, *The Anatomy of Melancholy*, part III, sec. 2, memb. 2, sub-sec. 1 (Everyman's Library), vol. III, p. 62.

37. *Ibid.*, part III, sec. 3, memb. 2; vol. III, p. 280.

38. *Ibid.*

39. Ford, *The Broken Heart*, act II, sc. 1; p. 211.

40. *Ibid.*, act III, sc. 2; p. 230.

41. *Ibid.*, act IV, sc. 2; p. 252.

42. *Ibid.*, pp. 254–255.

43. Giovanni's abnormal love-melancholy is quite analytically explained by Ford; but so intense is the portrayal of carnage resulting from the frustration of his passion for his sister that I hesitate to judge that his mental symptoms are "more pronouncedly emphasized" than the spectacle of carnage.

44. The recurrent skepticism of the early Jacobean playwright regarding the next world is given emphasis, for example, by the dying Bosola:

> O, I am gone:
> We are only like dead walls, or vaulted graves,
> That ruined, yield no echo.

(*Duchess of Malfi,* act V, sc. 5; Webster, *The Typical Elizabethan Plays,* ed. by Schelling and Black (3rd ed., 1949), p. 805.

BIBLIOGRAPHY

Historical Sources

Bowen, Thomas, *An Historical Account of Bethlehem Hospital.* London, 1783.

Brown, Tom, *London Amusements* (1700), ed. by Arthur L. Hayward. New York: Dodd, Mead & Co., 1927.

Harrison, G. B., *A Second Elizabethan Journal.* New York: Richard R. Smith, 1931.

———*A Third Elizabethan Journal.* London: Constable & Co., 1933.

Knight, Charles, *Cyclopedia of London.* London: C. Knight, 1851.

Lee, Sidney, "Bearbaiting, Bullbaiting, and Cockfighting," *Shakespeare's England.* Oxford: Clarendon Press, 1917; vol. II, pp. 428–436.

London, Corporation of, *Remembrancia.* London: E. J. Francis & Co., 1878.

Lupton, Donald, "London and the Countrey Carbonadoed" (1632), *Aungervyle Society Publications,* Second Series, No. XV. Edinburgh, 1883.

Memoranda Relating to the Royal Hospitals in London. London: Arthur Taylor, 1836.

More, Thomas, "The Four Last Things," *The English Works of Sir Thomas More;* ed. by W. E. Campbell. New York: The Dial Press, 1931.

O'Donoghue, Edward Geoffrey, *The Story of Bethlehem Hospital from its Foundation in 1247.* London: T. Fisher Unwin, 1914.

State Papers, Domestic Series. England: Reigns of Queen Elizabeth, King James I, and King Charles I.

Steele, Richard, *The Tatler,* no. cxxvii. London, January 31, 1709.

Stow, John, *A Survey of London* (1603); ed. by C. L. Kingsford. Oxford: Clarendon Press, 1908.

———*A Survey of London;* ed. and enlarged upon by John Strype, 6th ed. London: printed for W. Innys and J. Richardson, 1754.

Tuke, Daniel Hack, *Chapters in the History of the Insane in the British Isles.* London: Kegan Paul, Trench & Co., 1882.

Walsh, James J., "Nursing the Insane and Feebleminded," in *The History of Nursing.* New York: P. J. Kennedy & Sons, 1929.

Ward, Edward, *The London Spy.* London: printed monthly for J. Nutt, November 1698 to April 1700; collected and published, 1703.

Critical Works

Bowers, Fredson Thayer, *Elizabethan Revenge Tragedy.* Princeton: Princeton University Press, 1940.

Bright, Timothy, *A Treatise of Melancholie* (1586). The Facsimile Text. New York: Columbia University Press, 1940.

Bucknill, John Charles, *The Mad Folk of Shakespeare*. London: Macmillan & Company, 1867.

Burton, Robert, *The Anatomy of Melancholy* (1621); ed. by Floyd Dell and Paul Jordan-Smith. New York: Tudor Publishing Company, 1927 (editions: 1941, 1948).

——*The Anatomy of Melancholy* (1621). Everyman's Library. London: J. M. Dent & Sons, 1932.

——*The Anatomy of Melancholy* (1621). New edition. Boston: William Veazie, 1859.

Campbell, Oscar James, "What Is The Matter With Hamlet," *The Yale Review*, XXXII (1942), pp. 309–322.

Ellis-Fermor, U. M., *The Jacobean Drama*. London: Methuen & Co. Ltd., 1936.

Forest, Louise C. Turner, "A Caveat Against Invoking Elizabethan Psychology," *PMLA*, LXI (1946), pp. 651–672.

Freud, Sigmund, *A General Introduction To Psycho-Analysis*. New York: Liveright Publishing Corporation, 1935.

Guardia, J. M., *Essai Sur L'Ouvrage de Juan Huarte*. Paris: August Durand, 1855.

Hall, Joseph, *Satires* (1598). London: G. Willis, 1838.

Harrison, G. B., "Elizabethan Melancholy," introduction to Nicholas Breton's *Melancholike Humours*, ed. by Harrison. London: The Scholartis Press, 1929.

Jones, Ernest, "A Psycho-Analytic Study of Hamlet," *Essays in Applied Psycho-Analysis*. London: The International Psycho-Analytical Press, 1922; pp. 1–98.

Kerr, Mina, *The Influence of Ben Jonson on English Comedy*. New York: D. Appleton & Company, 1912.

King James, *Daemonologie* (1597); ed. by G. B. Harrison. London: The Bodley Head Ltd., 1924.

Machiavelli, Nicolo, *The Prince* (Elizabethan translation); ed. by Hardin Craig. Chapel Hill: University of North Carolina Press, 1944.

Marston, John, *The Scourge of Villanie* (1599); ed. by G. B. Harrison. New York: E. P. Dutton & Company, 1925.

Norden, John, *Vicissitudo Rerum* (1600). The Shakespeare Association Facsimiles, no. 4. London: Oxford University Press, 1931.

Peers, E. A., *Elizabethan Drama and its Mad Folk*. Cambridge: W. Heffer & Sons, Ltd., 1914.

Rowlands, Samuel, *The Letting of Humours' Blood in the Head-vein* (1600). Edinburgh: James Ballantine & Company, 1815.

Scot, Reginald, *The Discovery of Witchcraft* (1584). London: printed for A. Clark, 1665.

——*The Discovery of Witchcraft* (1584); ed. by B. Nicholson. London: E. Stock, 1886.

Sensabaugh, G. F., *The Tragic Muse of John Ford.* Stanford: Stanford University Press, 1944.

Somerville, Henry, *Madness In Shakespearean Tragedy.* London: The Richards Press Ltd., 1929.

Wells, H. W. *Elizabethan and Jacobean Playwrights.* New York: Columbia University Press, 1939.

Williamson, George, "Mutability, Decay, and Seventeenth Century Melancholy," *A Journal of English Literary History.* Baltimore: J. H. Furst Company, 1935; vol. II, pp. 121–150.

Wilson, F. P., *Elizabethan and Jacobean.* Oxford: Clarendon Press, 1946.

Vicary, Thomas, *The Anatomie of the Bodie of Man* (1548); ed. by F. J. and P. Furnivall. London: Early English Text Society, 1888.

Dramatic Works

Beaumont and Fletcher, *The Maid's Tragedy* (*c.* 1611); *Typical Elizabethan Plays,* ed. by F. E. Schelling and M. W. Black, 3rd ed. New York: Harper & Bros., 1949; pp. 699–748.

Chapman, George, *All Fools* (1605); *The Comedies and Tragedies of George Chapman,* ed. by R. H. Shepherd. London: John Pearson, 1873; vol. I, pp. 109–186.

——*An Humorous Day's Mirth* (1599); *The Comedies and Tragedies of George Chapman,* ed. by R. H. Shepherd. London: John Pearson, 1873; vol. I, pp. 49–108.

Chettle, Henry, *The Tragedy of Hoffman* (1603); ed. by A. F. Hopkinson. London: M. E. Sims & Company, 1917.

Dekker, Thomas, *The Honest Whore,* Part I (1604); *Thomas Dekker,* Mermaid Series, unexpurgated edition. London: T. Fisher Unwin, n.d.; pp. 89–190.

——*If This Be Not A Good Play, The Devil Is In It* (1612); *Dekker's Dramatic Works,* ed. by R. H. Shepherd. London: John Pearson, 1873; vol. III, pp. 259–360.

——*Match Me In London* (*c.* 1625); *Dekker's Dramatic Works,* ed. by R. H. Shepherd. London: John Pearson, 1873; vol. IV, pp. 129–216.

————*Westward Ho* (1607); *Dekker's Dramatic Works,* ed. by R. H. Shepherd. London: John Pearson, 1873; vol. II, pp. 279–363.

————and John Webster, *Northward Ho* (1607); *Dekker's Dramatic Works,* ed. by R. H. Shepherd. London: John Pearson, 1873; vol. III, pp. 1–80.

————John Ford, and William Rowley, *The Witch of Edmonton* (*c.* 1622); *Thomas Dekker,* ed. by E. Rhys, The Mermaid Series. London: T. Fisher Unwin, 1894; pp. 387–473.

Fletcher, John, *The Bloody Brother* (after 1616); *The Works of Mr. Francis Beaumont and Mr. John Fletcher.* London: printed for J. and R. Tonson and S. Draper, 1750; vol. V, pp. 81–171.

————*The Double Marriage* (*c.* 1620); *The Works of Mr. Francis Beaumont and Mr. John Fletcher.* London: printed for J. and R. Tonson and S. Draper, 1750; vol. VII, pp. 99–197.

————*The Mad Lover* (*c.* 1618); *The Works of Francis Beaumont and John Fletcher,* Variorum edition. London: Geo. Bell & Sons, 1908; vol. III, pp. 111–219.

————*The Nice Valour* (?). *The Works of Beaumont and Fletcher.* London: George Routledge & Sons, 1866; vol. II, pp. 454–472.

————*The Noble Gentleman* (1625?). *The Works of Beaumont and Fletcher.* London: George Routledge & Sons, 1866; vol. II, pp. 259–281.

————*The Pilgrim* (1621). *The Works of Beaumont and Fletcher.* London: Bradbury, Evans & Company (printers), 1840; vol. I, pp. 591–616.

————*The Pilgrim* (1621). *The Works of Mr. Francis Beaumont and Mr. John Fletcher.* London: printed for J. and R. Tonson and S. Draper, 1750; vol. V, pp. 439–527.

————*Rule A Wife, Have A Wife* (1624). *The Works of Francis Beaumont and John Fletcher,* Variorum edition. London: Geo. Bell & Sons, 1908; vol. III, pp. 357–464.

————*Valentinian* (*c.* 1612). *The Works of Francis Beaumont and John Fletcher,* Variorum edition. London: Geo. Bell & Sons, 1912; vol. IV, pp. 207–321.

————*The Wild Goose Chase* (1621). *Select Plays by Beaumont and Fletcher,* Everyman's Library. London: J. M. Dent & Sons, reprinted 1916; pp. 314–388.

————and William Shakespeare, *The Two Noble Kinsmen* (*c.* 1613); *The Complete Works of Shakespeare,* ed. by George Lyman Kittredge. New York: Ginn & Company, 1936; pp. 1409–1449.

Ford, John, *The Broken Heart* (1633); *John Ford,* ed. by Havelock Ellis. The Mermaid Series. London: T. Fisher Unwin, n.d.; pp. 182–282.

————*The Broken Heart* (1633); *Typical Elizabethan Plays,* ed. by F. E. Schelling and M. W. Black, 3rd ed. New York: Harper & Bros., 1949; pp. 897–942.

————*The Lover's Melancholy* (1628); *John Ford,* ed. by Havelock Ellis. The Mermaid Series. London: T. Fisher Unwin, n.d.; pp. 1–92.

————*Love's Sacrifice* (1633); *John Ford,* ed. by Havelock Ellis. The Mermaid Series. London: T. Fisher Unwin, n.d.; pp. 283–375.

————*Perkin Warbeck* (1634); *John Ford,* ed. by Havelock Ellis. The Mermaid Series. London: T. Fisher Unwin, n.d.; pp. 377–471.

————*'Tis Pity She's A Whore* (1633); *John Ford,* ed. by Havelock Ellis. The Mermaid Series. London: T. Fisher Unwin, n.d.; pp. 93–181.

Greene, Robert, *The History of Orlando Furioso* (1594). The Malone Society Reprints. London: Oxford University Press, 1907.

Jonson, Ben, *The Alchemist* (1610); *Ben Jonson,* ed. by Brinsley Nicholson and C. H. Herford. The Mermaid Series. London: T. Fisher Unwin, n.d.; vol. III, pp. 273–421.

————*Bartholomew Fair* (1614); *Ben Jonson,* ed. by C. H. Herford and Percy Simpson. Oxford: Clarendon Press, 1938; vol. VI, pp. 9–141.

————*The Devil Is An Ass* (1616); *Ben Jonson,* ed. by C. H. Herford and Percy Simpson. Oxford: Clarendon Press, 1938; vol. VI, pp. 155–269.

————*Every Man In His Humour* (*c.* 1598); *Typical Elizabethan Plays,* ed. by F. E. Schelling and M. W. Black, 3rd ed. New York: Harper & Bros., 1949; pp. 269–317.

————*Every Man Out Of His Humour* (1599); *The Complete Plays of Ben Jonson,* ed. by E. Rhys. Everyman's Library. London: J. M. Dent & Sons, n.d.; The Induction, vol. I, pp. 61–66.

————*The Poetaster* (1601); *The Complete Plays of Ben Jonson,* ed. by E. Rhys. Everyman's Library. London: J. M. Dent & Sons, n.d.; vol. I, pp. 233–307.

————*The Silent Woman* (1609); *Ben Jonson,* ed. by C. H. Herford and Percy Simpson. Oxford: Clarendon Press, 1937; vol. V, pp. 153–271.

Kyd, Thomas, *The Spanish Tragedy* (*c.* 1589); *Typical Elizabethan*

Plays, edited by F. E. Schelling and M. W. Black, 3rd ed. New York: Harper & Bros., 1949; pp. 41–89.

Marston, John, *Antonio and Mellida,* Part I (*c.* 1601); *The Plays of John Marston,* ed. by H. Harvey Wood. Edinburgh: Oliver and Boyd, 1934; vol. I, pp. 1–63.

————*Antonio and Mellida,* Part II, or *Antonio's Revenge* (1602); *The Plays of John Marston,* ed. by H. Harvey Wood. Edinburgh: Oliver and Boyd, 1934; vol. I, pp. 65–133.

————*Antonio and Mellida,* Part II, or *Antonio's Revenge* (1602); *The Works of John Marston,* ed. by A. H. Bullen. London: John C. Nimmo, 1887; vol. I, pp. 95–191.

————*The Malcontent* (*c.* 1602); *The Plays of John Marston,* ed. by H. Harvey Wood. Edinburgh: Oliver and Boyd, 1934; vol. I, pp. 135–215.

————*What You Will* (1607). *The Works of John Marston,* ed. by A. H. Bullen. London: John C. Nimmo, 1887; vol. II, pp. 317–419.

Massinger, Philip, *The City Madam* (1632). Princeton Studies in English No. 10, ed. by R. Kirk. Princeton: Princeton University Press, 1934.

————*The Duke of Milan* (1623); *The Plays of Philip Massinger,* ed. by W. Gifford, 3rd ed. Baltimore: J. W. Bond & Company, 1856; pp. 61–89.

————*The Maid of Honor* (1622); *The Plays of Philip Massinger,* ed. by W. Gifford, 3rd ed. Baltimore: J. W. Bond & Company, 1856; pp. 224–251.

————*A New Way To Pay Old Debts* (*c.* 1626); *Typical Elizabethan Plays,* ed. by F. E. Schelling and M. W. Black, 3rd ed. New York: Harper & Bros., 1949; pp. 849–896.

————*The Unnatural Combat* (*c.* 1621). Princeton Studies in English No. 7, ed. by R. S. Telfer. Princeton: Princeton University Press, 1932.

————*The Very Woman* (1634); *The Plays of Philip Massinger,* ed. by W. Gifford, 3rd ed. Baltimore: J. W. Bond & Company, 1856; pp. 438–466.

————*The Virgin Martyr* (1622); *Philip Massinger,* ed. by Arthur Symons. Mermaid Series. London: T. Fisher Unwin, n.d.; vol. II, pp. 283–380.

Middleton, Thomas, *A Mad World, My Masters* (1608); *The Works of Thomas Middleton,* ed. by A. H. Bullen. London; John C. Nimmo, 1885; vol. III, pp. 247–359.

————*The Roaring Girl* (1611); *The Works of Thomas Middleton,* ed. by A. H. Bullen. London: John C. Nimmo, 1885; vol. IV, pp. 1–152.

————*A Trick To Catch The Old One* (1608). *The Works of Thomas Middleton,* edited by A. H. Bullen. Boston: Houghton, Mifflin & Company, 1885; vol. II, pp. 247–352.

————and William Rowley, *The Changeling* (c. 1623); *Typical Elizabethan Plays,* ed. by F. E. Schelling and M. W. Black, 3rd ed. New York: Harper & Bros., 1949; pp. 807–848.

Shakespeare, William, *As You Like It* (c. 1600); *The Comedies of Shakespeare,* ed. by W. J. Craig. London: Oxford University Press, 1922; pp. 663–742.

————*Hamlet* (c. 1600); *The Tragedies of Shakespeare,* ed. by W. J. Craig. London: Oxford University Press, 1922; pp. 619–733.

————*Julius Caesar* (c. 1599); *The Tragedies of Shakespeare,* ed. by W. J. Craig. London: Oxford University Press, 1922; pp. 465–543.

————*King John* (c. 1596); *The Histories and Poems of Shakespeare,* ed. by W. J. Craig. London: Oxford University Press, 1922; pp. 1–79.

————*King Lear* (c. 1605); *The Tragedies of Shakespeare,* ed. by W. J. Craig. London: Oxford University Press, 1922; pp. 735–837.

————*Macbeth* (c. 1606); *The Tragedies of Shakespeare,* ed. by W. J. Craig. London: Oxford University Press, 1922; pp. 545–618.

————*Othello* (c. 1604); *The Tragedies of Shakespeare,* ed. by W. J. Craig. London: Oxford University Press, 1922; pp. 839–941.

————*Titus Andronicus* (c. 1593); *The Tragedies of Shakespeare,* ed. by W. J. Craig. London: Oxford University Press, 1922; pp. 215–292.

————*Twelfth Night* (c. 1601); *The Comedies of Shakespeare,* ed. by W. J. Craig. London: Oxford University Press, 1922; pp. 911–985.

Tourneur, Cyril, *The Atheist's Tragedy* (1611); *The Works of Cyril Tourneur,* ed. by Allardyce Nicoll. London: Fanfrolico Press, 1929; pp. 173–255.

————*The Revenger's Tragedy* (1607); *The Works of Cyril Tourneur,* ed. by Allardyce Nicoll. London: Fanfrolico Press, 1929; pp. 77–154.

Webster, John, *The Duchess of Malfi* (c. 1614); *Typical Elizabethan Plays,* ed. by F. E. Schelling and M. W. Black, 3rd ed. New York: Harper & Bros., 1949; pp. 749–806.

————*The White Devil* (1612); *The Complete Works of John Webster,* ed. by F. L. Lucas. New York: Oxford University Press, 1937; vol. I, pp. 103–192.

The Yorkshire Tragedy (*c.* 1606). Authorship uncertain. *The Shakespeare Apocrypha,* ed. by C. F. Tucker Brooke. Oxford: The Clarendon Press, 1918; pp. 249–261.

INDEX